THE DYNAMICS

OF

GODLY LEADERSHIP

Apostle Prophetess Rochelle Graham

Apostle Prophetess Rochelle Graham

The Dynamic of Godly Leadership

Published by One Faith Publishing

Richmond, VA. 23222

CONTENTS

DEDICATION. 1

FOREWORD 2

INTRODUCTION 4

CHAPTER I: LEADERSHIP AT ITS FINEST 5

CHAPTER II: THE WORLD IS WAITING ON YOU! 9

CHAPTER III: LEADING BY THE WISDOM OF GOD 18

CHAPTER IV: LEADING IN SYNC BY OBEDIENCE 33

CHAPTER V: THE ABILITY TO WORK WITH LESS (MORE WITH LESS) . . 51

CHAPTER VI: HOW GOD CHOOSES 56

CHAPTER VII: LEADERS UNDER INQUISITION 60

CHAPTER VIII: ULTIMATE POWER BELONGS TO GOD 70

CHAPTER IX: JUST A MISUNDERSTANDING. 76

CHAPTER X: KEEPING YOUR VOWS 83

CHAPTER XI: DANGEROUS TERMS OF YOUR VOWS 89

CHAPTER XII: THE POWER STRUGGLE 93

CHAPTER XIII: YOUR LEADERSHIP: MEMORABLE OR FORGETTABLE
. 98

CHAPTER XIV: WHEN LEADERS FOLLOW 105

CHAPTER XV: GODLY LEADERS ADHERE TO GODLY COUNSEL 111

CHAPTER XVI: DON'T LOSE IT 118

BIOGRAPHY OF APOSTLE PROPHETESS ROCHELLE GRAHAM 126

DEDICATION

This Book is first dedicated to God the Almighty Yahweh, as He is the giver of every good gift. I'm both humbled and honored to wear the garb of Author/Writer that has opened territorial gates of influence in my life. This influence has brought innumerable people in my path; thus, I secondarily dedicate this to the people my life has encountered and those whom I have had the honor of mentoring or leading over the previous decades. Those whom God was preparing to raise the next generation because the Lord placed in my heart the vision to fill the vast void that needed the wisdom of the Word.

It is with you that the words written herein will change the lives of thousands, even millions of people, as the power of knowledge is unleashed and the veils over their minds and destiny are lifted and removed.

There are too many of you to name, but knowing who you are will come to light as God anoints you and as He raises you up in your various nations to do what only you are assigned to do – your nation will never be the same. All of you that hail from the beautiful isles of the Bahamas, St. Lucia, Jamaica, Bermuda, Turks & Caicos all the way to the extensive continents of The United States of America and Canada have all been called with a great call – The Call To Greatness!

Your call to Greatness will pave the way for the Generations greater than you to emerge in the decades to come forth!

> *² As it is written in the prophets, Behold, I send my messenger before thy face, which shall prepare thy way before thee*
> *³ The voice of one crying in the wilderness, Prepare ye the way of the Lord, make his paths straight. Mark 1:2-3 (KJV)*

FOREWORD

The Dynamics of Godly Leadership
Written by: Apostle Prophetess Rochelle Graham

For a long time, it has been generally accepted to be true that, "*Everything rises, and falls based on LEADERSHIP!*" For this reason, there has been a great demand for individuals who can either identify or develop quality leaders who can be positioned at the helm of organizations or institutions with the capability of leading them to success.

Many would agree that the core principles of leadership are timeless and have remained true for leaders of all generations. However, it could be argued that some leadership principles that may be welcomed or even celebrated in secular entities are not deemed appropriate or applicable when an individual is given the responsibility of spiritual leadership. Because of this distinction, it is important for spiritual leaders to be reminded of the criteria of Heaven for their lives and leadership.

It is with this backdrop that God would choose to release a fresh download in this generation that would bring divine insight and instruction for what is to be defined as "godly leadership." As you begin to read the contents of this book, it will quickly become abundantly clear that Apostle Rochelle Graham is one of the persons that God has chosen to make a recipient of such a divine download. The clarity that she brings to the subject of godly leadership and the revelation she shares from the Word of God make it impossible for anyone to come in contact with this work and not leave challenged and changed.

Using the book of Judges as her study guide, along with insight from the Spirit of God, Apostle Graham makes plain the mission and mandate of godly leaders while pointing out some of the mistakes and missteps than one can make if they do not remain grounded in the One who has called and equipped them. She also guides the reader through the maze of maturation to help them to understand how God develops His leaders through the crucible of crisis.

Whether you are an emerging leader or one who has been giving Christian leadership for some time now, you will find here in these pages the inspiration and information you need to "level up" and become the best you can be. All too often, as leaders, we are pouring out into those around us to whom we have been assigned, but through this work, God has provided a fountain from which you can draw and be refreshed.

Over the past 30 years, I have had the wonderful privilege of teaching and mentoring leaders throughout the Bahamas and North America, and I have seen many of the truths shared in this work play out in the lives of leaders everywhere. In many instances, the mistakes that these leaders made were only because they lacked the lessons that Apostle Graham shares here in this work. I wish to commend her for her availability to God and for her faithfulness in doing the due diligence needed to make this divine download easily accessible and readily available to so many at such a critical time. My prayer is that God would bless Apostle Graham for her obedience, and may He continue to cause the rivers of Living Water to continue to flow through her to bring life to the masses.

I consider it an honor to have been given the opportunity to affirm publicly this phenomenal work and wish to say "Thank you" to this anointed vessel for the relationship we share. May God bless you, Bishop Brian Graham, and your entire family for the sacrifices they have made to allow you to do this work, and we look forward to what God will say and do through you next!

In His service,
Apostle Ivry Johnson (DD, M.O., J.P.)
Presiding Prelate
Koinonia Kingdom Network

INTRODUCTION

There are many versions when it comes to the opinion of what a leader is by definition. Yet definitively, there is line that is drawn to bring distinction to the type of leader that exists and what a Godly leader should ultimately be amid a world that seems to be devoid of it.

When it comes to leaders, the name from the Hebrew is, "**NAGID**", which means Chief or Commander. We all love the power that comes with the title of leader, but what about the weight of responsibility or the lines of accountability that must not be crossed in order to uphold Godly moral standards despite the fight against the *kosmoscrator* presence that seems to be winning over the masses?

This book outlines the '**Dynamics**' of what Godly leadership is and how it is to be implemented into the lives of leaders to stimulate spiritual growth and development and emit change in the process of maturing in Godly leadership.

This book takes a meticulous look into what the life of a Godly leader is by extracting from Godly examples as well as making avid deductions of what God leadership is not by looking at the outcomes of those leaders who got lost in their attempt to gain and fulfil the terms of their assignment and live out their God given mandates.

For this, we walk through the Book of "**The Judges**" – the chosen ones raised up to lead in a time when leaders were most needed!

CHAPTER I

LEADERSHIP AT ITS FINEST

Judges 5:2

*"For the leaders who took the lead in Israel,
For the people who volunteered [for battle], Bless the Lord!"*

When leaders lead, the people willingly offer themselves to the work of the one that stands out in front. Many desire the claim to fame, and that fame comes into the position of leadership, and many tend to bring with them parts of themselves that they should have long deserted or severed.

Let us start the conversation… not with what a leader is, but instead, what leadership is not.

Leadership is not:

- » Shouting imperative orders to others, trying to get them driven by fear to carry out your command.

- » Manipulating people by undermining, using subliminal suggestions that cause them to succumb under restraint.

- » Positioning yourself to be seen as the one in the light while you cast darkness over those that your leadership shadows.

- » Monopolizing the place of your position by believing you are the only one who can do the job, wanting to fortify 'a one man show'.

- » Dictating ungodly rules where you want other people to do things that you know are outside the parameters of moral soundness.

- » Being condescending in nature with others by treating them like they are beneath your level to be honored and/respected.

Leadership is using the voice of your influence to steer people in the right direction, or my personal definition... Leadership is using all spheres of your life's influence to bring effective change in others by expressing forward progressive movement from... **Shepherd to Sheep**

The Nature Of The Shepherd

- » A Shepherd must have the heart to:
- » Protect the spiritual sheep from (would be) predators.
- » Guide the spiritual sheep onto the right paths through the Word of God.
- » Keep the spiritual flock intact by teaching the power of unity as a whole.
- » Take care of the spiritual needs and natural needs based on resources.
- » Seek out the spiritual sheep that have wandered off no matter the extenuating circumstances.
- » Groom those who are ready to be promoted by showing them the way of servant leadership.

LEADERSHIP NOTES

LEADERSHIP NOTES

CHAPTER II

THE WORLD IS WAITING ON YOU!

> **Judges 5:7**
> *"The villagers ceased to be; they ceased in Israel, Until I, Deborah, arose,*
> *Until I arose, a mother in Israel"*

It is important for you to know there are some things that are:

- » Specific to your assignment
- » Designated to your destiny

This will not happen or manifest UNLESS you rise up and OBEY God – And do it!

Until You Arise

From this point, a referral will be made to the 'Godly leader', so by the time you have completed this reading, it will be embedded in your memory, your spiritual recall, and spirit. You are called to become a Godly leader!

- » A Godly leader never sees something that needs to be done and does not attend to it.
- » Does not bypass the situation because it is an opportunity to bring change.
- » Does not consider it insignificant or beneath you – kill haughtiness.
- » Does not delegate it to another person because it may require your imprint.

> *"My heart goes out to the commanders of Israel,*
> *The volunteers among the people; Bless the Lord!" Judges 5:9*

A Godly leader willingly offers themselves to the service of the people.

1. Be observant to their needs, both spiritual and natural.

Matthew 15:29-38

29 Jesus left there and went along the Sea of Galilee.
Then he went up on a mountainside and sat down.
30 Great crowds came to him, bringing the lame, the blind, the crippled,
the mute and many others, and laid them at his feet; and he healed them.
31 The people were amazed when they saw the mute speaking, the crippled made well, t
he lame walking and the blind seeing. And they praised the God of Israel.
32 Jesus called his disciples to him and said, "I have compassion for these people; they have
already been with me three days and have nothing to eat.
I do not want to send them away hungry,
or they may collapse on the way."
33 His disciples answered,
"Where could we get enough bread in this remote place to feed such a crowd?"
34 "How many loaves do you have?" Jesus asked.
"Seven," they replied, "and a few small fish."
35 He told the crowd to sit down on the ground.
36 Then he took the seven loaves and the fish, and when he had given thanks,
he broke them and gave them to the disciples, and they in turn to the people.
37 They all ate and were satisfied.
Afterward the disciples picked up seven basketfuls of broken pieces that were left over.
38 The number of those who ate was four thousand men, besides women and children

2. Attend to pertinent issues that are drastic and require immediate attention.

Mark 5:21-24

[21] *Jesus went back across to the other side of the lake.*
There at the lakeside a large crowd gathered around him.
[22] *Jairus, an official of the local synagogue, arrived,*
and when he saw Jesus, he threw himself down at his feet
[23] *and begged him earnestly, "My little daughter is very sick.*
Please come and place your hands on her, so that she will get well and live!"
[24] *Then Jesus started off with him.*
So many people were going along with Jesus that they were crowding him from every side.

3. Consider the best options before making a final decision on anything.

1 Samuel 24:8-22

[8] *Then David also got up afterward and went out of the cave and called after Saul, saying,*
"My lord the king!" And when Saul looked behind him,
David bowed with his face to the ground
and lay himself face down.
[9] *David said to Saul, "Why do you listen to the words of men who say,*
'David seeks to harm you?'
[10] *Behold, your eyes have seen today how the Lord had given you into my hand in the cave.*
Some told me to kill you, but I spared you; I said,
'I will not reach out my hand against my lord,
for he is the Lord's anointed.'
[11] *Look, my father! Indeed, see the hem of your robe in my hand! Since I cut off the hem of*
your robe and did not kill you, know and understand [without question]
that there is no evil or treason in my hands.
I have not sinned against you, though you are lying in wait to take my life.

¹² May the Lord judge between me and you;

and may the Lord avenge me on you; but my hand shall not be against you.

¹³ As the proverb of the ancients says,

'Out of the wicked comes wickedness'; but my hand shall not be against you.

¹⁴ After whom has the king of Israel come out?

Whom do you pursue [with three thousand men]?

A dead dog, a single flea?

¹⁵ May the Lord be the judge and render judgment between me and you;

and may He see and plead my cause and vindicate me by saving me from your hand."

¹⁶ When David had finished saying these words to Saul, Saul said,

"Is this your voice, my son David?" Then Saul raised his voice and wept.

¹⁷ He said to David, "You are more righteous and upright

[in God's eyes] than I; for you have done good to me, but I have done evil to you.

¹⁸ You have declared today the good that you have done to me,

for when the Lord put me into your hand, you did not kill me.

¹⁹ For if a man finds his enemy, will he let him go away [unharmed?

So may the Lord reward you with good in return for what you have done for me this day.

²⁰ Now, behold, I know that you will certainly be king

and that the kingdom of Israel will be established in your hand.

²¹ So now swear to me by the Lord that you will not cut off my descendants after me

and that you will not destroy my name from my father's household (extended family)."

²² David gave Saul his oath; and Saul went home,

but David and his men went up to the mountain stronghold.

David considered the options that were in his hands:

Option 1:   Kill King Saul and rid himself of an archenemy who conspired to destroy David and his chances of becoming the next King of Israel.

Option 2:   Allow King Saul to live and not extend his hand against God's anointed and remain guiltless in the entire matter, allowing God to deal with Saul personally.

David's final decision changed the trajectory of the entire situation:

- » **Personal Awareness** – Saul realized he had treated David badly while David treated him well, having the opportunity to kill him but opting not to do so.

- » **Humility/Repentance** – Saul repented of the evil that he had purposely intended against David that was rooted and driven by jealousy of David's battle winnings.

- » **Relationship Restored** – Saul fully understood God's position concerning David to be established as the next King of Israel and conceded to it without protest.

- » **Be The Solution** – By being firm about the best level of implementation and the reasoning behind it.

Nehemiah 4:21-23

21 So we carried on with the work with half of them holding spears
from dawn until the stars came out.
22 At that time I also said to the people, "Let each man with his servant spend the night
inside Jerusalem so that they may serve as a guard for us at night
and a laborer during the day."
23 So neither I, my brothers (relatives), my servants, nor the men of the guard who followed
me, none of us took off our clothes; each took his weapon [even] to the water.

Nehemiah was experiencing opposition and protest against the vision of the work that God assigned to him.

God gave him wisdom to handle the situation that would allow the work to continue and protect those that work by always being armed and anticipating a full launch of an attack from the enemy forces that were pressing for them to cease and desist in rebuilding the wall at Jerusalem.

From this passage, we can deduce that there is an important component of balance between work and war! Godly leader, as you obey God in your assignment, you will face opposition, and your position should be:

» Never engage in unnecessary verbal banter that will emit levels of chaos and confusion into your assignment.

» Never lose sight of the vision behind your assignment – keep it foremost in your thoughts and actions, so you do not lose sight of what God originally intended… by assigning it to you.

» Never underestimate the plots and devices of the enemy's forces and always be ready to war. For Nehemiah, he called for an actual physical war, but for us, we engage by the power of God in the spirit through prayer and disabling every artillery of the enemy and dismantling the plans of the wicked, bringing them down to naught.

» Never make the situation all about you.

Exodus 18:13-23

[13] *Now the next day Moses sat to judge [the disputes] the people [had with one another], and the people stood around Moses from dawn to dusk.*

[14] *When Moses' father-in-law saw everything that he was doing for the people, he said, "What is this that you are doing for the people? Why are you sitting alone [as a judge] with all the people standing around you from dawn to dusk?"*

[15] *Moses said to his father-in-law, "Because the people come to me to ask [about the will] of God.*

[16] *When they have a dispute they come to me, and I judge between a man and his neighbor and I make known the statutes of God and His laws."*

[17] *Moses' father-in-law said to him, "The thing that you are doing is not good.*

[18] *You will certainly wear out both yourself and these people who are with you, because the task is too heavy for you [to bear]; you cannot do it alone.*

[19] *Now listen to me; I will advise you, and may God be with you [to confirm my advice]. You shall represent the people before God. You shall bring their disputes and causes to Him.*

[20] *You shall teach them the decrees and laws.*

Moses was sitting in the seat as leader over the children of Israel, and as any good leader, he desired to be to them all that they needed him to be for every situation. What he did not understand is that putting himself in a place to be stressed and stretched was not going to prove profitable in either his life or the lives of the people he led.

God put Jethro, his father-in-law, in a position to see the danger of how Moses was handling the demands of the people who required him to sit as judge over every single happening among them. He spoke to and gave Moses good Godly advice – "Do not stress yourself out." Moses' eyes were opened as he began to see wisdom in Jethro's words:

- » Setting matters in levels of priority can bring new meaning to time management.
- » Setting others in positions of delegated authority under you can prove to be an asset.

It is important to remember that no man is an island, and that high demand on you, your time, and your anointing will lead to the deterioration of your ability to give to the masses all that they need of you.

Even Jesus needed the disciples in the areas of Food Distribution, Security& Crowd Control, and Ministers of Miracles among his people.

Becoming a Godly leader never comes with the mindset that it is all about you because the way God has set things up – it will never be just about you.

LEADERSHIP NOTES

LEADERSHIP NOTES

CHAPTER III

LEADING BY THE WISDOM OF GOD

To have the knowledge of what it means to be a leader – even a great leader is not enough. You need the Power of the Spirit of the Lord to rest upon you!

You need what we call in the 'old time church':

The Learning & The Burning

Head knowledge still requires the wisdom of God in order to impact people's lives positively.

Judges 6:27

27 Then Gideon took ten men of his servants and did just as the Lord had told him; but because he was too afraid of his father's household (relatives) and the men of the city to do it during daylight, he did it at night.

Gideon carried out the mission God gave him in the dark of night – by doing this, he was actually using wisdom in order to avoid contention and confusion. There are some things that God will assign you to do that are outside of people's knowledge or under the radar, merely to avoid their interference or hinder of the vision. It is always hard to hear but necessary to say that not everyone will be supportive of what God assigns you to do in the earth realm.

Unfortunately, the enemy assigns human agents against what God has purposed to accomplish among His people. It is of vital importance that you, as a Godly leader, maintain spiritual vigilance at all times to help minimize the opportunity for adversarial infiltration and to ensure you are equipped to complete your God given assignment.

Judges 6:36-40

36 Then Gideon said to God,

*"If You are going to rescue Israel through me, as You have spoken,
37 behold, I will put a fleece of [freshly sheared] wool on the threshing floor. If there is dew only on the fleece, and it is dry on all the ground [around it], then I will know that You will rescue Israel through me, as You have said."
38 And it was so. When he got up early the next morning and squeezed the dew out of the fleece, he wrung from it a bowl full of water.
39 Then Gideon said to God, "Do not let your anger burn against me, so that I may speak once more. Please let me make a test once more with the fleece; now let only the fleece be dry, and let there be dew on all the ground."
40 God did so that night; for it was dry only on the fleece, and there was dew on all the ground [around it].*

As a Godly leader, you need to know the difference and rightfully be able to decipher between hesitation, procrastination, and waiting on God's confirmation.

God never makes moves or decisions too quickly – there is an old song that says, "Only Fools Rush In". As leaders, we should always weigh the entirety of the matter before moving.

Second, ensure that you are in synchronization with the timing of God in making the right decision in the right time because it will play a role in the eventual happenings as you move toward completing our God given assignment.

How To Avoid Being Out of Sync:

» Ensure that what you heard was indeed from God by examining it by the weight of the Word – God is His Word, and when He speaks or gives directives, He will never go against that which He has already spoken in His Word.

» Ensure you are in the right season to move forward. Moving out of season can cause you to cast off your 'spiritual fruit' in the situation before time, deeming it unfruitful or useless.

» Ensure you are in sync with the timing of God. Even though God does not occupy time, time is important and relevant to the moves of God for His people. The correct timing can mean the difference between success and lack of progress.

» Ensure you are not being pressured by people or by extenuating circumstances. At times, people in their insistence that they are helping can apply undue and unnecessary pressure that can cause you to move before time and out of season. Always trust God by His Holy Spirit to lead you in the way that you should go – always!

Judges 6:34-35

[34] *So the Spirit of the Lord [f]clothed Gideon [and empowered him];*
and he blew a trumpet,
and the Abiezrites were called together [as a militia] to follow him.
[35] *He sent messengers throughout [the tribe of] Manasseh, and the fighting men were also called together to follow him; and he sent messengers to [the tribes of] Asher, Zebulun, and Naphtali, and they came up to meet them.*

When God gave Gideon his assignment, he also gave him the ability to draw the resources that he needed along with the people that he would need in order to accomplish his God given assignment. God knew that Gideon could not accomplish this great feat singlehandedly, so He put the plan in place and caused it to come together the minute that Gideon accepted what had to be done.

God will always give you what you need to ensure you have success on your Assignment/Mission.

People will follow a leader:

a. **That has a vision that is clear and forthright** – Tell the people plainly what you are trying to do and your plan behind accomplishing the vision with no hidden agendas.

b. **That has strength and fortitude in making good decisions** – People will be skeptical about a leader who either takes too long to make good decisions or one who makes numerous erroneous decisions.

c. **That shows their level of submission to God** – There is power behind submission – as you submit to God's instruction and authority, God will cause those that you lead to submit unwaveringly to your level of authority.

d. **That has a good name and reputation** – There is a past to everyone's existence, but your character changes when you come into your rightful seat of authority – the old passes away and the new emerges. A good name that can be trusted will go further than one with a shady character.

e. **That has a heart for the people they lead** – People react better to leaders with whom they can connect and when they can identify the qualities of a caring leader, even if they are in the sea of the masses of people. The heart of the leader can be seen through the words that he/she uses and the way they treat those connected to their life and vision.

f. **That know God on an intimate level** – True worshippers make awesome leaders because they know God intimately and desire the things of God more than anything else – they place God as a priority, and in so doing, those they lead tend to do the same. True Worshippers birth True Worshippers!

g. **That is trustworthy and confidential** – Being a vault when it comes to handling sensitive information means all the difference in leading. Keep the secrets a secret!

There are three (3) important attributes of a good leader. Let's talk about them:

Character

» Mental and moral qualities distinctive to an individual.

» A Godly leader's mind has to be in the right place in God because what emanates from the mind will affect your morals:

> ### Proverbs 23:7
> *For as he thinks in his heart, so is he [in behavior—one who manipulates].*

This scripture is saying so plainly that, whatever you entertain in your mind, you will eventually act it out in your behavior, and there is no way around that. It's the way we were made.

Thus, it is so important to keep a balance on what you allow to be accessed by your mind because, after processing, there will be a moment of release that can cause irrefutable damage to the lives of the people that you are called to lead.

> ### Romans 8:5-6
> [5] *For those who are living according to the flesh set their minds on the things of the flesh [which gratify the body], but those who are living according to the Spirit,*
> *[set their minds on]*
> *the things of the Spirit [His will and purpose].*
> [6] *Now the mind of the flesh is death [both now and forever—because it pursues sin]; but the mind of the Spirit is life and peace [the spiritual well-being that comes from walking with God—both now and forever];*

It is solely up to you to become a Godly leader and to make a conscientious decision to live either according to the flesh or according to the Spirit – to do so could mean the difference between saving a life or being a stumbling block to those who need a Godly influence in their lives.

Sometimes being who we are, naturally, can be damaging especially when the people we are leading are expecting more from us on a Godly and Spiritual level.

> ### Colossians 3:2
>
> *2 Set your mind and keep focused habitually on the things above [the heavenly things], not on things that are on the earth [which have only temporal value].*

There are fleshly habits to break, and there are Spiritual habits to make. A good habit to formulate is to remain focused on the Word of God, the Kingdom of God, and refrain from entertaining thoughts that, if not contained, could lead to focusing on temporal worldly things that lead to eventual decay of Godly moral standards.

> ### Philippians 4:8
>
> *8 Finally, [believers, whatever is true, whatever is honorable and worthy of respect, whatever is right and confirmed by God's word, whatever is pure and wholesome, whatever is lovely and brings peace, whatever is admirable and of good repute; if there is any excellence, if there is anything worthy of praise, think continually on these things [center your mind on them, and implant them in your heart].*

Here is your guideline plain and simple… You have the choice of what your mind is allowed to entertain. As a Godly leader, you will have one opportunity to make a good, Godly first impression.

As a leader, you never want to be caught in a moment when you had your mind centered on the wrong things that led to bring shame to the Kingdom of God because, if you allowed those things, whatever they could be, to be implanted in your heart – then out of the state of the heart, your mouth made a public announcement that could lead to the downfall of Ministry or devastation of your God given Vision.

> ### Romans 12:2
>
> *2 And do not be conformed to this world [any longer with its superficial values and customs], but be [c]transformed and progressively changed [as you mature spiritually] by the renewing of your mind [focusing on godly values and ethical attitudes], so that you may prove [for yourselves] what the will of God is, that which is good and acceptable and perfect [in His plan and purpose for you].*

Being transformed by the Word of God allows for progressive change in your spiritual life, a change that will impact all facets of your life for good. The key to this is holding fast to Godly morals and always pressing to do the right thing and not going along with the majority rule numbers, even if that means standing alone in your place of ethical excellence – do so and make your Father God, the One who called you, so very proud of your stance.

> ### 2 Corinthians 10:5
> **5** *We are destroying sophisticated arguments and every exalted and proud thing that sets itself up against the [true] knowledge of God, and we are taking every thought and purpose captive to the obedience of Christ,*

Sometimes people in leadership do not want to admit it, but it is often their thoughts that "mess them up" and cause them to make decisions that impact the lives of the people they lead negatively.

According to this scripture, you retain the right and power to destroy internal arguments that try to rise up and create friction against the purpose of God and your obedience to Him. Take a hold of those thoughts and put them in subjection until they are powerless to overtake you.

Credibility

The quality of being trust-worthy and believed in:

» Trustworthiness

» Reliability

A Godly leader has to endeavor to win the 'heart' confidence of the people they lead, or their level of leadership will be futile and ineffective. The people have to be able to count on you no matter the number of people you are leading.

> ### Proverbs 19:22
> *That which is desirable in a man is his loyalty and unfailing love,*
> *But it is better to be a poor man than a [wealthy] liar.*

As a Godly leader, you can never negate the position of your loyalty first to God and then to the people that God has assigned to your life. The accompany to your loyalty is your unfailing love – Agape – that gives you the strength to love even those we categorize as 'unlovable', those that are built to test the parameters of your love and leadership.

You will not be exempt from having to experience people in the vastness of who they are and the things they will do. But remember, God is always looking for your response to them. The fact of the wrong they may have done or said will not matter, only your Godly response to them and the situation.

Proverbs 11:13

He who goes about as a gossip reveals secrets.
But he who is trustworthy and faithful keeps a matter hidden.

Never be named among the sect of people who take pleasure in being what it takes to obtain the secret but not having the fibers of faithfulness that it takes to keep the matter in a place of confidential discretion. And as a Godly leader, you need to keep a distance between you and those that assemble around you that have the "Gift of Gossip" – it will hurt your Ministry.

Over time, you will find that the lips that can hold nothing will be the same lips that will have a 'tell all' session regarding your life. Beware of the gossipers and do not allow that spirit to get a foothold; otherwise, the enemy will have access to create a stronghold that is harder to uproot and rout out.

Proverbs 10:9

He who walks in integrity and with moral character walks securely,
But he who takes a crooked way will be discovered and punished.

Integrity is always going to be the order of the day for a Godly leader – there are no exceptions in this instance, and upholding moral right is the only path to be taken to ensure you will never have to sit in the seat of God's judgement for making a decision without integrity that had the capacity to bring shame.

> ### Titus 2:7
> *⁷ And in all things show yourself to be an example of good works,*
> *with purity in doctrine [having the strictest regard for integrity and truth], dignified.*

Above everything else in your life, as a Godly leader, you are called to be an example to the people you lead – they will adopt your ways and begin to do things as they see you do. So never take your position lightly because the spotlight is always on you, and remember, as you lead, they are led by the Spirit of the Lord.

> ### Zechariah 8:16-17
> *¹⁶ These are the things which you should do: speak the truth with one another;*
> *judge with truth and pronounce the judgment that brings peace in*
> *[the courts at] your gates.*
> *¹⁷ And let none of you devise or even imagine evil in your heart against another,*
> *and do not love lying or half-truths; for all these things I hate,' declares the Lord."*

God hates liars, and He wants absolutely nothing to do with those who perpetuate lie after lie. God wants the Word of the Lord in our mouths to produce truth. No matter the situation, always remember God's position. God wants us to speak truth and not fall in love with telling lies that overtake your life because lying can become a habit before you even realize it.

Charisma

- » Compelling attractiveness or charm that can inspire devotion in others.
- » A Godly leader comes with an innate ability to draw people.
- » The light of God in you draws people.
- » The salt of God in you savors the lives of people.

So, if we are to be the light, how is it that so many people are 'dimmers' and use a switch of some sort to turn up and turn down their light based on so many given factors, like mood, pressure, or uncontrolled circumstances?

Being the salt of the earth, we are to be adding flavor to the lives of God's people by showing them that serving God is an experience of a lifetime.

So how is it that so many are serving up whatever they feel instead of what the Word of God outlines?

Dimmer Switches

» Personal life issues that spill over into Ministry and/or business.

» Placing everything else other than God and your assignment as priority.

Unsavory Flavors

» The words that come forth are tearing down the people that they were intended to build up and establish.

» The neglect of making the correct kind of preparation, for instance studying the Word of God or ensuring what is needed is in place and is not left to chance – give of your best always to the service of the Lord.

» The design of God is for you to empower the people that you are called to lead, those who are to be greater than you in their calling, and do not discourage them based on envy or hidden agenda. Always ensure that your words are in-tune with the Word of the Lord and relevant to the time in which you are living.

To be charismatic in any sphere is to step out of the box…

Hebrews 6:1

Therefore, let us get past the elementary stage in the teachings about the Christ, advancing on to maturity and perfection and spiritual completeness, [doing this] without laying again a foundation of repentance from dead works and of faith toward God

---

Years ago, I attended a church where every Sunday we heard the same message of Salvation. It was after service on one of those Sundays that I stopped to ask my then Pastor a pertinent question, "Pastor, since we are all Believers here in this church, what happens after Salvation?

And would it not be better to begin to teach the church members how to maintain their Salvation?" It must have dropped a bomb on my Pastor because he never answered me!

He was stuck in a box. A box of a single message… Salvation. He had no clue how to get the people that he was leading to the next level in their relationship or walk with God. He was stuck in a box… A box of not having the knowledge to build a team of leaders who would be trained and stand in the place of the five-fold ministry.

This scripture encourages us to move past the elementary or infancy stage of being stuck on the same old message but to grow and mature into perfection and completeness. God never intended for us to be stuck or to become stuck; instead, He wants charismatic thinkers, those who will allow him to elevate our minds so He can speak to our hearts and cause us to affect change in the earth realm.

Acts 2: 7-12
7 They were completely astonished, saying,
"Look! Are not all of these who are speaking Galileans?
8 Then how is it that each of us hears in our own language or native dialect?
9 [Among us there are] Parthians, Medes and Elamites, and people of Mesopotamia,
Judea and Cappadocia, Pontus and Asia [Minor],
10 Phrygia and Pamphylia, Egypt and the districts of Libya around Cyrene,
and the visitors from Rome, both Jews and proselytes (Gentile converts to Judaism),
11 Cretans and Arabs—
we all hear them speaking in our [native] tongues about the mighty works of God!"
12 And they were beside themselves with amazement and were greatly perplexed,
saying one to another, "What could this mean?"

Believe it or not, you have it in you to cause people who see the Works of God in you to be left in amazement, and this is just the way the Lord wants it to be said of you – never ordinary….EXTRAORDINARY!

Too often, truly called and anointed leaders are passed over for those who are pushed to the forefront because of partiality and undue favor from the Pastor who expressed wrongly, which usually leads to chaos and confusion in Ministry.

Put yourself in a place never to be passed over or left to the side because you are called, chosen, and anointed with great purpose. You are that light set on a hill, and God wants to use your light to draw those outside the Kingdom on the inside to experience His love, power, and mercy. You are a portion of a greater plan, and all you have to do is make yourself available for God to position and use you in a powerful way!

1 Corinthians 12:7

7 But to each one is given the manifestation of the Spirit
[the spiritual illumination and the enabling of the Holy Spirit] for the common good.

Here is your confirmation! You have been spiritually illuminated; to be illuminated is to be "lighted up." You have a built-in LED that is set on high beam no matter the situation or circumstance because the Holy Spirit has already enabled you with what you need to accomplish great exploits in the earth realm.

Ephesians 4:10-14

10 He who descended is the very same as
He who also has ascended high above all the heavens,
that He [His presence] might fill all things [that is, the whole universe]).
11 And [His gifts to the church were varied and] He Himself appointed some as apostles
[special messengers, representatives], some as prophets [who speak a new message from God
to the people], some as evangelists [who spread the good news of salvation],
and some as pastors and teachers [to shepherd and guide and instruct],
12 [and He did this] to fully equip and perfect the saints
(God's people) for works of service, to build up the body of Christ [the church];
13 until we all reach oneness in the faith and in the knowledge of the Son of God,
[growing spiritually] to become a mature believer, reaching to the measure of the fullness of
Christ [manifesting His spiritual completeness and exercising our spiritual gifts in unity].

You are part of a Body, and when you get in your place in the Body, it will cause the Body to work perfectly. God's plan for the church is that it would be fully outfitted and not left to chance. Your works in the Kingdom of God are purposed to build up the people of God, people who need what you are bringing to the table.

It is so important for you to understand that, as you lead, you will still need people. You will need other leaders to support you as you mature and come into the fullness of all that God has called for you to be in Him.

Charisma is unique to every individual leader, and your spiritual gifts are a supernatural enablement that God gives you, and they are released through you as they would never be released through any other person.

LEADERSHIP NOTES

LEADERSHIP NOTES

CHAPTER IV

LEADING IN SYNC BY OBEDIENCE

Judges 7:2

Then the Lord said to Gideon, "There are too many people with you for Me to hand over Midian to them, otherwise Israel will boast [about themselves] against Me, saying, "My own power has rescued me."

Whenever God does anything, He does so with exhibiting the power and might of His supernatural hand in mind. He did this with Gideon. He cut down the number of men assigned to accompany Gideon in battle just to prove it was not the power of their numbers that would win the victory, but it was His hand of power.

Gideon obeyed God down to the very detail. He did as he was commanded by God, and his obedience led him to the victory that shut the mouths of his enemies.

When you are obedient to the mandate of God over your life, it puts you in "SYNC."

Being in sync will cause all the resources that you need to execute your assignment to come to you in abundance.

Your Ministry will find itself in the place of the overflow with:

- » People
- » Resources
- » Investments

There is no leader that would turn people away on any given Sunday should their seating capacity hit maximum; instead, they would opt to call for additional seating to accommodate the addition. Numbers are not the only factor that indicates success on any Ministry level; however, it is a factor.

There are 34 scriptures in total that reference a crowd following Jesus.

Here are just a few of those scriptures:

Luke 14:25

²⁵ Now large crowds were going along with Jesus;

Mark 5:24

*²⁴ And Jesus went with him; and a large crowd followed Him
and pressed in around Him [from all sides].*

Mark 10:1

*Getting up, He left there (Capernaum) and went to the region of Judea and beyond the
Jordan; and crowds gathered around Him again and accompanied Him,
and as was His custom, He once more began to teach them.*

Luke 5:1

*Now it happened that while Jesus was standing by the Lake of Gennesaret (Sea of Galilee),
with the people crowding all around Him and listening to the word of God*

Matthew 4:25

*²⁵ Large crowds followed Him from Galilee and the [d]Decapolis and Jerusalem
and Judea and the other side of the Jordan.*

Matthew 8:1

When Jesus came down from the mountain, large crowds [a]followed Him.

Each one of these verses indicate that there was a crowd that followed Jesus, there was something about him that drew crowd after crowd after crowd!

The 'Crowd' is defined as a large number of people gathered in an unruly way, leaving little or no room for movement. Most have never seen a crowd, and some never will because of their heart and disposition. There has to be an anointing that flows uncontaminated and uncompromisingly, an anointing that draws people from everywhere for one God ordained purpose.

God always draws people by purpose on purpose!

Ministry in Overflow

  » People

People are the most valuable blessings as you're establishing yourself as a Godly leader. God watches to ascertain how leaders will treat those that he has given them to lead.

The first thing to recognize is that "the people" do not and will never belong to you. They fully and will always belong to God.

From the 'Genesis', God made mankind (both male and female) so that He could have a reflection of Himself in the earth realm, a realm He created and gave them to have dominion over, but God never anticipated that Pastors or spiritual leaders would dominate or manipulate His people. Eventually, mankind grew in numbers, and where there are mass numbers, there will always arise the need for leaders.

Leaders have their place, but Godly leaders can never get caught up in seeing people as chattel. If so, that would automate that the leaders are slave masters. Slave masters endorse the mentality that "I am in charge" and you do as I say or suffer the consequences.

To be a Godly leader, you must change your perception and see people as God sees them, precious and in need of nourishment, cultivation, and a connection to a life-giving source – God.

Your mission as a leader under God is that you nourish them with the love of God, cultivate them with the knowledge of God, and connect them to the Father God through life giving principles of the Word.

Cultivate the lives of the people you lead by teaching and living the truth of the Word of the Lord. The best Godly leader is one who leads by (God's Word) example.

> ### 2 Timothy 4:2
>
> *2 Preach the word [as an official messenger]; be ready when the time is right and even when it is not [keep your sense of urgency, whether the opportunity seems favorable or unfavorable, whether convenient or inconvenient, whether welcome or unwelcome]; correct [those who err in doctrine or behavior], warn [those who sin], exhort and encourage [those who are growing toward spiritual maturity], with inexhaustible patience and [faithful] teaching.*

The position of Godly leadership warrants a list that some may find taxing at best, but it is an essential part of spiritual development, which is necessary to you in all areas, so there will be no shortfalls as it pertains to your pattern of leadership.

According to this scripture, a Godly leader is mandated to:

- » Preach – Proclaim the Word of the Lord as the Lord has detailed.
- » Ready – To correct, exhort, and encourage God's people.
- » Exhibit – Hold fast to inexhaustible patience and be faithful in teaching the Word of God.

> ### Acts 20:28
>
> *28 Take care and be on guard for yourselves and for the whole flock over which the Holy Spirit has appointed you as overseers, to shepherd (tend, feed, guide) the church of God, which He bought with His own blood.*

One of the major areas of development as a leader emerges when you have to learn how to bring sync in the area of being guard.

First, take every precaution to avoid being ensnared by the enemy or getting caught up in unscrupulous dealings.

Second, guard the people in which you have been called to shepherd.

It may come easier to some to handle and guard themselves, but the base of leadership broadens when you have to take responsibility over others. You can never make the final decision for them; however, you can set a premier example that your leading is all they need to walk in the right way and make the right decisions the first time. Keep watch!

Jeremiah 3:15

[15] *"Then [in the final time] I will give you [spiritual] shepherds after My own heart, who will feed you with knowledge and [true] understanding.*

In order for any leader to feed others with knowledge and true understanding, they must first grasp knowledge and understanding for themselves. So when you combine the formula of wisdom, it will begin to work through you and into the lives of the people you are leading.

Being in the final end-time, you cannot afford to take time or your call for granted, and do not be overcome by thoughts that convey that you are not the right choice or that you do not have what it takes to secure the seat of leadership and make a difference.

Ephesians 4:11-12

[11] *And [His gifts to the church were varied and] He Himself appointed some as apostles [special messengers, representatives], some as prophets [who speak a new message from God to the people], some as evangelists [who spread the good news of salvation], and some as pastors and teachers [to shepherd and guide and instruct],*
[12] *[and He did this] to fully equip and perfect the saints (God's people) for works of service, to build up the body of Christ [the church];*

God gave various gifts to the Body of Christ to make the inclusion that there is a position for everyone. There are no two people alike on the planet. Even identical twins have varying and notable differences and DNA, and there most certainly is no one made like you to do what God has ordained for you to do.

You must come in sync with the gifts of God in you and position your heart to receive God's instruction so that, whenever He speaks to you, you will be ever willing to obey His every command.

To be in sync with God, you must love Him more than anyone or anything else in this world. You must put everything else aside and embrace all that God is by making a covenant to remain unrelentingly faithful to God by being your authentic self and no one else.

There are, at times, a manifestation of the "copycat" in tiers of leadership. People see the prosperity and success of other leaders and want to mimic what they are witnessing. But what they are missing is the person they are admiring (hopefully not envying) has become so prosperous and successful because they gave the best of who they are and remained true to their authentic self.

Note: To all up and coming Godly leaders. Be true to God and authentic to self – anything else will cause you to face the disappointment of not ending up on the same route of success.

Titus 1:5-9

5 *For this reason I left you behind in Crete, so that you would set right*
what remains unfinished, and appoint [a]elders in every city as I directed you,
6 *namely, a man of unquestionable integrity, the husband of one wife,*
having children who believe, not accused of being immoral or rebellious.
7 *For the overseer, as God's steward, must be blameless, not self-willed, not quick-tempered,*
not addicted to wine, not violent, not greedy for dishonest gain [but financially ethical].
8 *And he must be hospitable [to believers, as well as strangers], a lover of what is good,*
sensible (upright), fair, devout, self-disciplined [above reproach—
whether in public or in private].
9 *He must hold firmly to the trustworthy word [of God] as it was taught to him,*
so that he will be able both to give accurate instruction in sound [reliable, error-free]
doctrine and to refute those who contradict [it by explaining their error].

The standards of the systems of the world are never to be held in the same regard as the standards of God as it relates to leadership. By the world's standards, there are no rules to excelling – do what you have to do in order to get what you want, but in the Kingdom of God, unscrupulous rules do not apply.

All Godly leaders must live their lives in sync with the standards of God and never live them out as if they are the "sub-standard." When you live a life in order, it becomes easy to emit order as you lead others. There will be no undermining for power, only the upright and ethical dealings of leaders who fear God and refute error on all levels. God's way is the only way – One standard!

Ezekiel 34:1-10

And the word of the Lord came to me, saying,

² "Son of man, prophesy against the shepherds of Israel. Prophesy and say to them, the [spiritual] shepherds, 'Thus says the Lord God, "Woe (judgment is coming) to the [spiritual] shepherds of Israel who have been feeding themselves!
Should not the shepherds feed the flock?
³ You eat the fat [the choicest of meat], and clothe yourselves with the wool, you slaughter the best of the livestock, but you do not feed the flock.
⁴ You have not strengthened those who are weak, you have not healed the sick, you have not bandaged the crippled, you have not brought back those gone astray, you have not looked for the lost;
but you have ruled them with force and violence.
⁵ They were scattered because there was no shepherd, and when they were scattered they became food for all the predators of the field.
⁶ My flock wandered through all the mountains and on every high hill; My flock was scattered over all the face of the earth and no one searched or sought them."''
⁷ Therefore, you [spiritual] shepherds, hear the word of the Lord:
⁸ "As I live," says the Lord God, "certainly because My flock has become prey, My flock has even become food for every predator of the field for lack of a shepherd, and My shepherds did not search for My flock, but rather the shepherds fed themselves and did not feed My flock;

The point here is quite direct. God's judgment comes on those who take advantage of the people they are leading by placing their personal needs first. In so doing, they cause a dispersion where the people are abandoning the House of God because of the undue actions of a failed leader. No one is perfect, but we are to strive for perfection in the things of God so that we can do what we are assigned by God to do without any infractions of reproach being noted against us.

Resources

Resource is defined as – stock or supply of money or other assets that can be drawn on by a person or organization in order to function effectively.

The long and short of the entire matter is resources, especially monetary, are a necessary component to proficient and effective function of Ministry.

Gone are the days when people gave total devotion to their church and submitted their time, talent, and treasure freely without a cheque stub attached to it.

Today, the churches of this modern day, no matter the denominational attachment, only recognize the power of the dollar ($) sign. All major inferences in every meeting in Ministry concern money – the use of it, the needs, or the lack thereof.

And one of the biggest mistakes that Ministry leaders make in the course of trying to handle the responsibilities that go along with the assignment is beginning to see the people they are assigned to lead, not as people, but as dollar ($) signs. They get lost in the lines of doing what needs to be done by seeing the people as the ends to the means, when they should never lose focus on the One that gave them the initial assignment – God! For He alone has the resources to bring them all that is necessary for the efficient and proficient management of Ministry.

A leader who is God oriented does **NOT** see the people who gathered and assembled to worship God as a potential dollar ($) sign!

Genesis 22:14

So Abraham named that place The Lord Will Provide. And it is said to this day, "On the mountain of the Lord it [will be seen and provided.

When Abraham was faced with dealing with the most perplexing decision he had ever had to make in his life – he moved forward in FAITH trusting God for all that he needed God to provide. He moved forward in obedience even though the evidence pointed to him losing the one thing God had promised to give him – his son.

He found out that, at the end of the day, God Will Provide exactly what you need when you need it, no matter what. Remember, all things originate with God, and He alone has the final say on EVERYTHING!

A Godly leader looks to God to provide for the Vision and the Mission that He has gifted them to complete. Yes, it is a gift! A gift-given opportunity to do something great in the Kingdom of God that NO ONE ELSE can do, ONLY YOU! Thus, one must trust God's ability to bring the blessings and to release it in such enormous proportions that what is given by the Ministry supporters will pale in comparison to His outpour.

2 Corinthians 9:8

And God is able to make all grace [every favor and earthly blessing] come in abundance to you, so that you may always [under all circumstances, regardless of the need] have complete sufficiency in everything [being completely self-sufficient in Him] and have an abundance for every good work and act of charity.

There are three little words that have the power to shift your life when your faith excels in God, and they are "God Is Able." When your faith comes in alignment with these three words, you will see nothing as impossible, undoable, or difficult because you will have an assurance in the Resource Source that God is in your personal life and in the extension of Ministry through you!

Be always confident that God alone is the Source of your every Resource and that, in all circumstances, He will ensure that all that is needed and made available upon your demand.

God never intended for Abraham to lose the Promise (his son Isaac), but through the experience, he learned that 'God Is Able To Provide', and from that one encounter, he learned by FAITH that he could trust God to supplement his life on all levels.

For every Godly leader, there will be an encounter that thereafter, a new level of faith will be enacted where one can believe God for anything and everything. This is called, **NEXT LEVEL FAITH**!

Hebrews 13:5

Let your character [your moral essence, your inner nature] be free from the love of money [shun greed—be financially ethical], being content with what you have; for He has said, "I will never [under any circumstances] desert you [nor give you up nor leave you without support, nor will I in any degree leave you helpless], nor will I forsake or let you down or relax My hold on you [assuredly not]!"

The problem with the majority of spiritual leaders who find the circle of success in Ministry is, many times, they get caught up in the 'HAVING', which eventually eats away at their moral fibers, and they begin to allow their earthly possessions and allowances to take precedence over their spiritual assignment, and they convolute spiritual things so that they can have access to more money, houses, cars, and earthly possessions by insisting it's their inherent right.

Being blessed is the portion of every Believer, but when blessings begin to take over your life, it replaces the face of the Blesser and (God) Himself in levels of importance in your life, and it begins to spill over into the place of Ministry. Then a line has been crossed, and spiritual assessment and prioritization is necessary in order to restore and equate responsibility and accountability of Ministry.

In order to avoid this erroneous path, there must be an open line to Central – a Prayer Life. Every Godly leader needs a prayer life that is definitively set on keeping them in the place of humility where the "havings" are not placed above the "doings" of the assignment of God.

As well as for the maintenance of *Ministry vs. Personal* Life, where the true and real struggles are emitted. Prayer will keep the hearts of Godly leaders pure towards God, and the Spirit of the Lord will be able to move freely to give direction and instruction as deemed necessary.

As a Godly leader, be careful about becoming closed, that you place the methodology of God to bring the provision in a box. Remember, God is your ultimate resource, and His provision will always be greater than money.

I Timothy 6:17

Command those who are rich in this present age not to be haughty,
nor to trust in uncertain riches but in the living God, who gives us richly all things to enjoy.

Sometimes there are untapped resources around us, but we are too focused on one thing or one area to see it. I challenge you as a God-believer to broaden your spiritual insight regarding new levels of resources.

Investments

Investment is defined as "the action or process of investing money for profit or material result."

For some reason, the church has been set in a cycle when it comes to financial management that has, over time, proven itself to be unproductive and unfruitful.

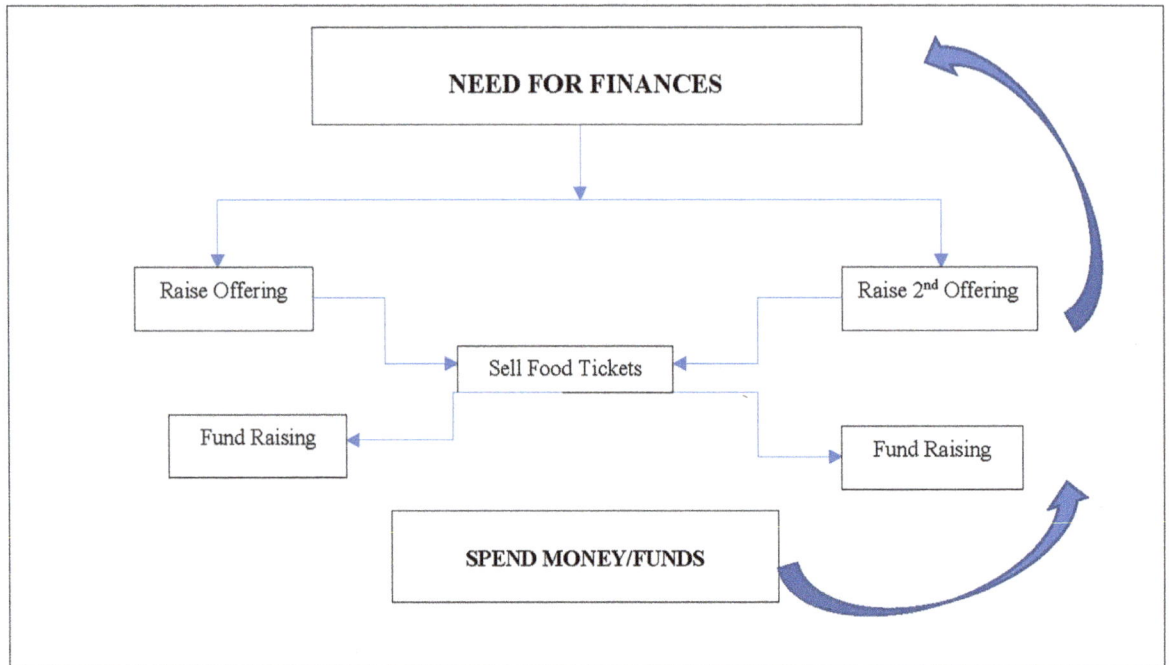

God wants us as Godly leaders to be wise concerning finances, and a part of financial wisdom is Investment by taking a portion of what you have stored up and/or saved and putting it in a financial market to yield for a greater return. Whatever God puts in your hand, with it, He has placed the capacity to multiply and create supplementary amounts that will generate wealth in the Kingdom of God.

Matthew 25:14-30

"For it is just like a man who was about to take a journey,
and he called his servants together and entrusted them with his possessions.
¹⁵ To one he gave five talents, to another, two, and to another, one,
each according to his own ability; and then he went on his journey.
¹⁶ The one who had received the five talents went at once and traded with them,
and he [made a profit and] gained five more.
¹⁷ Likewise the one who had two [made a profit and] gained two more.
¹⁸ But the one who had received the one went
and dug a hole in the ground and hid his master's money.
¹⁹ "Now after a long time the master of those servants returned
and settled accounts with them.
²⁰ And the one who had received the five talents came and brought him five more, saying,
'Master, you entrusted to me five talents. See, I have [made a profit and]
gained five more talents.
²¹ His master said to him, 'Well done, good and faithful servant. You have been faithful
and trustworthy over a little, I will put you in charge of many things;
share in the joy of your master.'
²² "Also the one who had the two talents came forward, saying,
'Master, you entrusted two talents to me. See, I have [made a profit and]
gained two more talents.
²³ His master said to him, 'Well done, good and faithful servant. You have been faithful
and trustworthy over a little, I will put you in charge of many things;
share in the joy of your master.'
²⁴ "The one who had received one talent also came forward, saying, 'Master, I knew you to
be a harsh and demanding man, reaping [the harvest] where you did not sow
and gathering where you did not scatter seed.
²⁵ So I was afraid [to lose the talent],
and I went and hid your talent in the ground. See, you have what is your own.'

²⁶ "But his master answered him,
'You wicked, lazy servant, you knew that I reap [the harvest]
where I did not sow and gather where I did not scatter seed.
²⁷ Then you ought to have put my money with the bankers,
and at my return I would have received my money back with interest.
²⁸ So take the talent away from him, and give it to the one who has the ten talents.'
²⁹ "For to everyone who has [and values his blessings and gifts from God,
and has used them wisely],
more will be given, and [he will be richly supplied so that] he will have an abundance; but
from the one who does not have
[because he has ignored or disregarded his blessings and gifts from God],
even what he does have will be taken away.
³⁰ And throw out the worthless servant into the outer darkness; in that place
[of grief and torment]
there will be weeping [over sorrow and pain] and grinding of teeth
[over distress and anger].

God is that Master who entrusts His possessions into the hands of his Beloved servants, and He gives to everyone on different levels of blessings, based on the Master's choice of distribution. The Master could have given the same amount of Talents to all the servants, but he gave based on what He saw in each of the servants.

And the end result caused each servant to see what the Master actually saw in them. Their actions spoke volumes and proved what was in their heart, as well as their level of expertise in handling finances.

God's ultimate reasoning behind providing, especially in the area of finances, is **NOT** so that we can live in that binding cycle of **'NEEDING FINANCES to RAISING FUNDS to SPENDING FUNDS'** and having to start that cycle all over again. That cycle propagates poverty and keeps the Body of Christ bound in their level of thinking and understanding regarding the **PURPOSE** of money.

The first two servants took the finances they were given, and they TRADED them and made a PROFIT that manifested financial increase. Never be limited in your thinking concerning the way God wants you to view money. It is not only for people in the world to create wealth through investment.

God wants the Church and His people to be stepping into that arena, so the Kingdom of God can advance in the earth, and the cost of carrying the Gospel can be financed.

For some of you, this is shocking information that God does not want the Pastors having to beg the congregation for funds to send Missionaries into the fields to evangelize and win souls for the Kingdom of God. The Church should be in such a financially stable place that, when any need arises, the provision is already in place because PLANNING preceded the need.

God gives us responsibility and thereafter comes the demand of accountability, where God Himself will **RECONCILE** the account that you were entrusted with from the beginning. The question here is, what response are you going to give if you have not advanced past the **CYCLE OF POVERTY**?

Any leader who has been walking in this way and had people following them will have to answer to God for their formidable ways… "Did you not think?" God wants us to be thinkers, shakers, and movers! It's time to invest to build and create wealth in all spheres of life. This will show those who do not believe that Believers are not just TAKERS, but they are planners and provisionally responsible people.

This passage scripture, Matthew 25:14-30, was the first course in Money

Management – and only two out of three passed.

In today's market, one (1) Talent of Gold would be worth $1,400,116.57. What an opportunity to do something profound by making an investment! The first servant traded and doubled his investment; the second moved in like wisdom as the first and traded on the Money Market and doubled his initial investment.

So now, here is your opportunity to see what **NOT** to do…. The third servant took the one (1) Talent and dug a hole and buried it. He allowed fear to bury his opportunity to make an investment that could have changed his life and status.

He allowed fear to cause him to fail to use wisdom even to bank it. He ended up falling out of favor with his master and losing the one (1) talent he was initially given.

From the monetary standpoint, investments can build wealth so that Ministry efforts can be stabilized and local outreaches and initiatives funded without unnecessary strain on the congregation.

By doing so, you can become that pillar of blessing to the people who have been committed to stand in loyalty over the years. After all, Ministry is about building up God's people.

No Godly leader should be cheap, mean, or selfish. Their hearts should be geared toward coming up with creative and innovative ideas to bless the people that they have been assigned to lead. It is always a good time to level up and begin to do something to bring profit to the Kingdom of God. Remember, when you HAVE more, you can DO more!

LEADERSHIP NOTES

LEADERSHIP NOTES

CHAPTER V

THE ABILITY TO WORK WITH LESS (MORE WITH LESS)

Judges 7:7

And the Lord told Gideon, "With the three hundred men who lapped I will rescue you, and will hand over the Midianites to you. Let all the other people go, each man to his home."

God, at times, will put leaders in a place where they have to do more with less! Many will beg to differ because the majority often feel that overwhelming success can only be denoted in massive crowd numbers, when in fact, God by His supernatural power can enact any level of override and make the numbers factor obsolete.

To do more with less, especially when working the arms of Ministry:

1. Shows the leader that he/she has the God given ability to do with less – which implies total trust and reliance on God.

2. Shows that God wants to manifest the demonstration of His power among his people.

3. Shows the importance of allowing God to get the Glory from everything that we do in the Kingdom.

Even in the positions of leaders who have passed the position of the novice, self will always try to stand up and show off itself. Why? Because of the innate desire to prove the worthiness of your level of leadership. But the truth is, when you yield to God's plan and decide to do things God's way, everything you put your hand forward to do:

- » Planning events
- » Appointing leaders
- » Choosing new locations
- » Deciding on expansion
- » Dealing with hard issues

Your ability in God's hands will always prove fruitful – In Judges 7:7 God did not want Gideon as a novice, being new to leadership, to get lost in a world of his own works or plan. So God devised a strategy to do MORE with LESS!

Yes, there is power in numbers. We have heard it said in all arenas of life, but when God is standing with you, He is ONE equated to the power of numbers. It is important for it to be interjected as a point of an imperative fact to the heart of every Godly leader who has been called to get the job done with less than anticipated…

"DO NOT PANIC!"

Do not panic when you are working on Kingdom building expansion projects or outreaches and you are short on manpower and low on resources. Just hold fast to the Memo: God is and has the Master Plan!

As a leader, the only thing you need to be focused on is building your level of faith and falling back completely and unreservedly on the Arms of God. You are going to find that, just like Gideon, it is only the **CORE PEOPLE** that you need standing with you in the times of the battle. In those times, you cannot call on everybody, only those who are:

- » **Ready to accredit God with the victory.**

God does not like 'show-offs' – the same way they show off with material things, they will show off when they do anything in and/or for the Kingdom of God, whether that is praying for someone or giving the largest amount as a donation to the Ministry.

» **Quality people in the fabric of their spiritual life to support your leadership.**

A lesson worth learning is, you better choose quality over quantity every day, because quantity can bring with it levels of chaos and confusion that can lead to upheaval and to the detriment of a thriving Ministry.

At first glance, numbers may appear impressive, but with the interjection in one area of weakness, the CORE PEOPLE could easily lose their footing and the bond of unity that you thought would last a lifetime would break.

Always be girded and guarded in your movements as a Godly leader.

» **Committed to the strategy that God gives you as leader**

You will need to choose those who will receive with humility the instruction of God through you as leader. Not those who question and at every opportunity try to interject to change the original plan that God gave you to follow.

Now, let me clarify. I am not saying that you as leader should take the position as 'know it all' but never deviate from the heart of what God gave you to do. After all, God gave you the Vision, and He will hold you accountable for deviating from what He originally intended. Always remember, there are many routes and methods to implementation depending on what you are trying to do in and for the Ministry.

LEADERSHIP NOTES

LEADERSHIP NOTES

CHAPTER VI

HOW GOD CHOOSES

Judges 7:4

Then the Lord said to Gideon, "There are still too many people; bring them down to the water and I will test them for you there. Therefore it shall be that he of whom I say to you, 'This one shall go with you,' he shall go with you; but everyone of whom I say to you, 'This one shall not go with you,' he shall not go."

God's perception on who should be chosen to walk with you in Ministry is always completely different to how we would opt to choose people. In verse 4, God told Gideon, if I say he goes – he goes; if I say he does not go – he does not go!

As a Godly leader, you need to finetune your ear to God so that you will not make the wrong selection or select someone for the wrong reasons.

Most of the time, leaders do not take the time to seek God or wait on His answer and approval before appointing their CORE PEOPLE in positions in Ministry, and this can bring far-reaching repercussions that can hurt in more ways than one over time.

Remember – ONLY the CORE PEOPLE went with Gideon!

You cannot afford to take any shortcuts when it comes to the selection process. Yes, you may be needing help/ hands in the Ministry, but the wrong hands in the wrong place can only bring wrong results.

For most leaders, after they have come to sit in the seat of leadership for a while, they feel they have it all down packed, to the place that, when people come into the Ministry, they take out their roll of 'sticky labels' and label them based on what they see – and this can be damaging and can result in people feeling judged by making premature decisions to leave based on one leader's unscrupulous action.

Leaders, you are never to take for granted that the enemy wants to infiltrate the church, and he waits for the opportunity when your guard is down.

The following gives you direct pointers on how not to choose your core people – those who will stand with you to undergird you and have the victory positions of the Ministry as their priority under God.

1. **Never choose based on "the look" – because there needs to substance beyond the looks.**

Those who look the part are rarely carrying the package of power that God is requiring to walk with you in Ministry.

2. **Never choose based on the amount that a person is capable of giving into your Ministry.**

Those people who are blessed to give will always have an air of genuine humility – not superiority. As a leader, you need to be able to discuss and decipher in order to make the right choice.

3. **Never choose based on their prior Ministerial portfolio because they may be running from fire but still carrying cinders that can kindle and light a world of confusion and misunderstanding in your Ministry.**

Choose a person who has a good name and reputation in God. This person will bless any House of God – but you must ensure the person is on their God assignment and not running from their God ordained mandate because it will result in upheaval and chaos.

Always put everything before God in prayer and get God's clearance. God has the final say – NOT YOU!

LEADERSHIP NOTES

LEADERSHIP NOTES

CHAPTER VII

LEADERS UNDER INQUISITION

And the men of [the tribe of] Ephraim said to Gideon, "What is this thing that you have done to us, not calling us when you went to fight with Midian?"
And they quarreled with him vehemently. **Judges 8:1**

As a leader, you will find that there will be times, even when you are walking in total obedience to God, those that are supposedly a part of the Ministry Vision will bring under question your decisions to leave them out of the big picture. You need to have full assurance that, as you make decisions in obedience to God, not to be swayed by the voices of the general concerns or mass persuasion.

Beyond what you can see in the natural realm, God knows the end from the beginning; thus, any exclusions He makes is necessary. God is omniscient; thus, you must trust Him to lead and guide you, especially in those varying and difficult situations.

Psalm 32:8
"I will instruct you and teach you in the way you should go;
I will counsel you with my eye upon you"

To many people, it may appear that they are pre-qualified over everyone else, and that mentality alone makes them negligible for great moves by God in your Ministry.

God always choses on purpose the least unlikely people to lead and accomplish great feats for the Kingdom of God. This way, His Power and Wisdom can be sighted first, and He can have full acclaim and Glory out of the situation.

God usually chooses persons who don't quite *fit the bill*. That's why he chose you!

David

A shepherd boy with no army or tactical training overcame and defeated a giant, named Goliath. God used David to set the stage before the entire world that the God of Israel has all power to defeat giants, even by the hands of the unmastered novice.

1 Samuel 17:45-58

[45] *David said to the Philistine, "You come against me with sword and spear and javelin, but I come against you in the name of the Lord Almighty, the God of the armies of Israel, whom you have defied.*

[46] *This day the Lord will deliver you into my hands, and I'll strike you down and cut off your head. This very day I will give the carcasses of the Philistine army to the birds and the wild animals, and the whole world will know that there is a God in Israel.*

[47] *All those gathered here will know that it is not by sword or spear that the Lord saves; for the battle is the Lord's, and he will give all of you into our hands."*

[48] *As the Philistine moved closer to attack him, David ran quickly toward the battle line to meet him.*

[49] *Reaching into his bag and taking out a stone, he slung it and struck the Philistine on the forehead. The stone sank into his forehead, and he fell facedown on the ground.*

[50] *So David triumphed over the Philistine with a sling and a stone; without a sword in his hand he struck down the Philistine and killed him.*

[51] *David ran and stood over him. He took hold of the Philistine's sword and drew it from the sheath. After he killed him, he cut off his head with the sword. When the Philistines saw that their hero was dead, they turned and ran.*

⁵² Then the men of Israel and Judah surged forward with a shout and pursued the
Philistines to the entrance of Gath[f]
and to the gates of Ekron. Their dead were strewn along
the Shaaraim road to Gath and Ekron.
⁵³ When the Israelites returned from chasing the Philistines, they plundered their camp.
⁵⁴ David took the Philistine's head and brought it to Jerusalem;
he put the Philistine's weapons in his own tent.
⁵⁵ As Saul watched David going out to meet the Philistine, he said to Abner, commander of
the army, "Abner, whose son is that young man?" Abner replied,
"As surely as you live, Your Majesty, I don't know."
⁵⁶ The king said, "Find out whose son this young man is."
⁵⁷ As soon as David returned from killing the Philistine,
Abner took him and brought him before Saul,
with David still holding the Philistine's head.
⁵⁸ "Whose son are you, young man?" Saul asked him.

David said, "I am the son of your servant Jesse of Bethlehem."

Moses

Who was exposed to governmental leadership then raised up to become a human rights activist and spiritual leader over millions? God chose Moses because he knew that, through all the grueling trials, he would be glorified among the children of Israel through Moses' stance of obedience and humility under God's hand.

Exodus 3:1-21

Now Moses was tending the flock of Jethro his father-in-law, the priest of Midian,
and he led the flock to the far side of the wilderness and came to Horeb,
the mountain of God.
² *There the angel of the Lord appeared to him in flames of fire from within a bush.*
Moses saw that though the bush was on fire it did not burn up.
³ *So Moses thought, "I will go over and see this strange sight—*
why the bush does not burn up."
⁴ *When the Lord saw that he had gone over to look, God called to him from within the*
bush, "Moses! Moses!" And Moses said, "Here I am."
⁵ *"Do not come any closer," God said.*
"Take off your sandals, for the place where you are standing is holy ground."
⁶ *Then he said, "I am the God of your father,*[a] *the God of Abraham, the God of Isaac and*
the God of Jacob." At this, Moses hid his face, because he was afraid to look at God.
⁷ *The Lord said, "I have indeed seen the misery of my people in Egypt.*
I have heard them crying out because of their slave drivers,
and I am concerned about their suffering.
⁸ *So I have come down to rescue them from the hand of the Egyptians and to bring them*
up out of that land into a good and spacious land, a land flowing with milk and honey—
the home of the Canaanites, Hittites, Amorites, Perizzites, Hivites and Jebusites.
⁹ *And now the cry of the Israelites has reached me,*
and I have seen the way the Egyptians are oppressing them.
¹⁰ *So now, go. I am sending you to Pharaoh to bring my people the Israelites out of Egypt."*
¹¹ *But Moses said to God,*
"Who am I that I should go to Pharaoh and bring the Israelites out of Egypt?"
¹² *And God said, "I will be with you.*
And this will be the sign to you that it is I who have sent you:
When you have brought the people out of Egypt, you will worship God on this mountain."

¹³ Moses said to God, "Suppose I go to the Israelites and say to them,
'The God of your fathers
has sent me to you,' and they ask me, 'What is his name?' Then what shall I tell them?"
¹⁴ God said to Moses, "I am who I am.[c]
This is what you are to say to the Israelites: 'I am has sent me to you.'"
¹⁵ God also said to Moses, "Say to the Israelites, 'The Lord, the God of your fathers
—the God of Abraham, the God of Isaac and the God of Jacob—has sent me to you.'
"This is my name forever, the name you shall call me from generation to generation.
¹⁶ "Go, assemble the elders of Israel and say to them, 'The Lord, the God of your fathers—
the God of Abraham, Isaac and Jacob—appeared to me and said:
I have watched over you and have seen what has been done to you in Egypt.
¹⁷ And I have promised to bring you up out of your misery in Egypt into the land of the
Canaanites, Hittites, Amorites, Perizzites, Hivites and Jebusites—
a land flowing with milk and honey.'
¹⁸ "The elders of Israel will listen to you. Then you and the elders are to go to the king of
Egypt and say to him, 'The Lord, the God of the Hebrews, has met with us.
Let us take a three-day journey
into the wilderness to offer sacrifices to the Lord our God.'
19 But I know that the king of Egypt will not let you go unless a mighty hand compels him.
²⁰ So I will stretch out my hand and strike the Egyptians with all the wonders
that I will perform among them. After that, he will let you go.
²¹ "And I will make the Egyptians favorably disposed toward this people,
so that when you leave you will not go empty-handed.
²² Every woman is to ask her neighbor and any woman living in her house for articles of
silver and gold and for clothing, which you will put on your sons and daughters.
And so you will plunder the Egyptians."

The enemy will cause many to rise up against you as you take a stand to obey God in your assignment. There are those who will defy and rebel against your leadership and implement insurrections designed to destroy you before you get the full grasp of the Vision. Nonetheless, do not be moved by enemy plots and know that God will always give you the knowledge, wisdom, and spiritual skill to gain the tactical advantage and cause you to subdue those that rise up against you.

God has all **POWER,** and he will never fail to use His power to defend His children!

Jesus

Came to the earth to become the Savior of the world – but not born into a family of high notable estate or of governmental influence. Instead, He was born into a family of moderate means and income, in a stable and coddled in a lowly manger. God chose a part of Himself to birth in His people reliance on Him as their God, thus instituting right relationship.

Luke 2:4-21

⁴ So Joseph also went up from the town of Nazareth in Galilee to Judea, to Bethlehem the town of David, because he belonged to the house and line of David.
⁵ He went there to register with Mary,
who was pledged to be married to him and was expecting a child.
⁶ While they were there, the time came for the baby to be born,
⁷ and she gave birth to her firstborn, a son. She wrapped him in cloths and placed him in a manger, because there was no guest room available for them.
⁸ And there were shepherds living out in the fields nearby,
keeping watch over their flocks at night.
⁹ An angel of the Lord appeared to them,
and the glory of the Lord shone around them, and they were terrified.
¹⁰ But the angel said to them, "Do not be afraid.
I bring you good news that will cause great joy for all the people.
¹¹ Today in the town of David a Savior has been born to you; he is the Messiah, the Lord.

12 This will be a sign to you: You will find a baby wrapped in cloths and lying in a manger."

13 Suddenly a great company of the heavenly host appeared with the angel,

praising God and saying,

14 "Glory to God in the highest heaven,

and on earth peace to those on whom his favor rests."

15 When the angels had left them and gone into heaven, the shepherds said to one another,

"Let's go to Bethlehem and see this thing that has happened,

which the Lord has told us about."

16 So they hurried off and found Mary and Joseph, and the baby,

who was lying in the manger.

17 When they had seen him, they spread the word concerning

what had been told them about this child,

18 and all who heard it were amazed at what the shepherds said to them.

19 But Mary treasured up all these things and pondered them in her heart.

20 The shepherds returned, glorifying and praising

God for all the things they had heard and seen, which were just as they had been told.

21 On the eighth day, when it was time to circumcise the child,

he was named Jesus, the name the angel had given him before he was conceived.

The Father God longs for intimate relationship with His people but, even more so, with those whom He has chosen to stand in the realm of leadership, so the place and power of their influence can be under His direct control and guidance system. Every Godly leader should strive to obtain and maintain intimate connection with God. It will keep you walking in His ways and prevent you from making any unnecessary mistakes in crucial areas.

1 John 2:3-6

Now by this we know that we know Him, if we keep His commandments. He who says, "I know Him," and does not keep His commandments, is a liar, and the truth is not in him. But whoever keeps His word, truly the love of God is perfected in him. By this we know that we are in Him. He who says he abides in Him ought himself also to walk just as He walked.

God desires that we:

> » **KNOW** Him!

To be aware of who He is as our God and spend time with Him to develop a relationship with Him.

> » Are **IN** Him!

To be completely grafted into him and have our nature perfected through living out the love of God in the earth.

> » **ABIDE** in Him!

To become the embodiment of the nature and character of God and live a life that demonstrates that completely.

And this, in fact, proves and verifies that Godly leaders can live a life that is above sin and not make excuses like so many others that often say, "I am only human."

To know God is to be in Him, and abiding in Him empowers you to live that right relationship with God boldly, just as God originally intended.

LEADERSHIP NOTES

LEADERSHIP NOTES

CHAPTER VIII

ULTIMATE POWER BELONGS TO GOD

> ### Judges 9:2-4
>
> ² *"Speak now in the hearing of all the leaders of Shechem,*
> *'Which is better for you, that seventy men,*
> *all of the sons of Jerubbaal rule over you, or that one man rule over you?' Also, remember*
> *that I am your own bone and flesh."*
> ³ *So his mother's relatives spoke all these words concerning him so that all the leaders of*
> *Shechem could hear; and their hearts were inclined to follow Abimelech, for they said,*
> *"He is our relative."*
> ⁴ *And they gave him seventy pieces of silver from the house of Baal-berith,*
> *with which Abimelech hired worthless and undisciplined men,*
> *and they followed (supported) him.*

Godly leaders must live out the standard of "Do", especially when choosing people to walk with you in leadership.

Here, we see Abimelech's desire to sit in the seat of power and poise, but he lacked a level of diplomacy and selecting skills. He made a good campaign by swaying his uncles to convince the majority of the family that he was the best person to be chosen as leader.

He made a *"Self-Recommendation."* He was saying to them, it doesn't get any better than this… **I am the ONE!** This proves that he was all about self-promoting and self-exaltation, and that recipe will always be one headed for disaster. You will find that the spirit of self-promotion, self-exaltation, and self-adoration is always accompanied by hidden agendas and subverted motives that will be revealed in the eventuality of things taking place.

His campaign won; however, for him that was not enough, so he sought out those who stood in a place to eradicate those who had the authority to remove and/or replace him. He was taking no chances on losing that which he had tried with all his might to attain.

This is why it is so important to **wait on POSITIONING** from God because it will not come with the burden of having to press and stress to persuade people to follow you – it will manifest, and leading will come with ease of passage, the way God intended!

Abimelech found some derelict gangsters for hire to go on his mission with him to kill all of his brothers – all seventy of them – except one. His strategy was to wipe them all out and destroy them, so the ultimate control and the ultimate power could rest with him. Literally, he was operating with an undermining spirit. He displayed insidious behavior, the kind that is never indicative of men and women of God who desire to lead.

Godly leaders should never try to push themselves to the front of the line based on the fact that they feel they are rightfully deserving or not – they simply humble themselves and wait for their turn in the lineup to lead. Follow the ways of the Lord in the Word and your name will be called sooner rather than later.

It is so very important to remember that God has all power to promote, and all the earth efforts of man will pale in comparison to when God himself says. "Yes, now it is your time!"

> **Psalm 127:1-2**
> *¹Unless the Lord builds the house, They labor in vain who build it;*
> *Unless the Lord guards the city, The watchman keeps awake in vain.*
> *²It is vain for you to rise early, To retire late,*
> *To eat the bread of anxious labors—For He gives [blessings] to His beloved even in his sleep.*

God's efforts and capabilities will outweigh you on every turn, and you never want to be left or named as the one who tried to excel, promote, or move to the next level without God.

Based on the definitive origin of his name, Abimelech was called to lead – his name means "Leader of a King"; however, his methodology was left to question because he could not get past his own desires to be great.

He felt the capacity and the ability he innately possessed coupled with his strong desires to sit in the seat of leadership, but he went about it the wrong way. And the worst thing about it, he hired wicked accomplices who were down for whatever based on the financial favor he extended to them.

A leader with an undermining spirit will do absolutely anything with no regard to morals or scruples just to get ahead or to take the place of the advantage.

God desires that we remain supportive in our roles as leaders and with a mind to show people that, no matter who opposes your leadership, you can overcome by the Power of God and not the works of your flesh.

Hebrews 6:10

[10] For God is not unjust so as to forget your work and the love which you have shown for His name in ministering to [the needs of] the saints (God's people), as you do.

It is said here, clearly for all to see and understand that God will never forget all the good of what you do in the Kingdom, and He will reward you accordingly. The design of God's heart speaks to who he is – **GOD IS A REWARDER!**

Hebrews 13:16

Do not neglect to do good, to contribute [to the needy of the church as an expression of fellowship], for such sacrifices are always pleasing to God.

God loves when we freely make notable sacrifices without having to be probed or pushed, and in this, God is pleased with you. When God is pleased with you, there will be nothing impossible for you and no good thing withheld from you.

John 15:13

[13] No one has greater love [nor stronger commitment] than to lay down his own life for his friends.

The heart of a Godly leader should be sown in all that is good, and he/she ought to be willing to have the heart and mind to lay down their lives for the good of those that they lead and never be the one with the design to destroy them in any way.

Philippians 2:4

⁴ Do not merely look out for your own personal interests, but also for the interests of others.

This instruction is clear and needs no clarification or re-evaluation. Personal interests are always good because you do not want to let yourself go, but the inclusion of the interest is even better. Give the best of yourself and lose the appeal of self-interest so that you will be free to hear God and obey, and you will never get caught up in self because in the flesh dwells nothing good.

Abimelech had a great desire and passion to lead, but he was unsuitable. He is proof that self-promotion leads to ruin.

LEADERSHIP NOTES

LEADERSHIP NOTES

CHAPTER IX

JUST A MISUNDERSTANDING

Judges 11:14-21

¹⁴ *But Jephthah sent messengers again to the king of the Ammonites,*

¹⁵ *and they said to him, "This is what Jephthah says:*
'Israel did not take the land of Moab or the land of the Ammonites.

¹⁶ *For when they came up from Egypt,*
Israel walked through the wilderness to the Red Sea and came to Kadesh;

¹⁷ *then Israel sent messengers to the king of Edom, saying, "Please let us pass through your land," but the king of Edom would not listen. Also they sent word to the king of Moab, but he would not consent. So Israel stayed at Kadesh.*

¹⁸ *Then they went through the wilderness and went around the land of Edom and the land of Moab, and came to the east side of the land of Moab, and they camped on the other side of the [river] Arnon; but they did not enter the territory of Moab, for the Arnon was the [northern] boundary of Moab.*

¹⁹ *Then Israel sent messengers to Sihon king of the Amorites, king of Heshbon, and Israel said to him, "Please let us pass through your land to our place."*

²⁰ *But Sihon did not trust Israel to pass through his territory;*
so Sihon gathered together all his people and camped at Jahaz and fought against Israel.

²¹ *The Lord, the God of Israel, gave Sihon and all his people into the hand of Israel, and they defeated them; so Israel took possession of all the land of the Amorites, the inhabitants of that country.*

Jephthah was a natural born leader, but because of the disposition of his birth, he was cast out as a derelict by those in connection to his bloodline. Most of the time, those who are cast out are the ones who are truly called of God to accomplish great things in the earth realm.

The reason for Jephthah being treated in this manner was because of the flaw of being born to a woman from the wrong side of town – his mother was a prostitute. And to them, that implicated that his right of access and inheritance to the family was tainted.

But his family soon found out that Jephthah was the one they truly needed in order to defeat their surrounding enemies.

They would have to abolish their pride and fall at the mercy of the one they had deemed 'good for nothing'. In the Bahamas, there is a colloquial name for someone like that – '**POTCAKE** – they only know me when they need me! *(Song by Phil Stubbs, Bahamas)*

Judges 11:6-8

⁶ and they said to Jephthah, "Come and be our leader,
so that we may fight against the Ammonites."
⁷ But Jephthah said to the elders of Gilead, "Did you not hate me and drive me
from the house of my father? Why have you come to me now when you are in trouble?"
⁸ The elders of Gilead said to Jephthah, "This is why we have turned to you now: that you
may go with us and fight the Ammonites and become head over
all the inhabitants of Gilead."

From '**Cast Out**' to '**Commander**'!!!! God changed the title of his name and reputation overnight! Jephthah's family had to swallow their pride and run to the one whom God had anointed to the solution to the militant uprising they were facing.

To you, the leader reading this book: "You are the SOLUTION (the means of dealing with and solving difficult situations) to the uprising issues around you – locally, nationally and globally."

> ## Matthew 21:42-44
>
> [42] *Jesus asked them, "Have you never read in the Scriptures: 'The [very] [a]Stone which the builders rejected and threw away, Has become the chief Cornerstone; This is the Lord's doing, And it is marvelous and wonderful in our eyes'?*
> [43] *Therefore I tell you, the kingdom of God will be taken away from you and given to [another] people who will produce the fruit of it.*
> [44] *And he who falls on this Stone will be broken to pieces; but he on whom it falls will be crushed."*

For Jephthah, his destiny had indeed taken on a life that manifested into him being that very stone – being cast away and rejected, and then by the Hand of God, he was given power to become a force to be reckoned with as a leader of a nation.

He accepted their proposal on his terms of negotiation. He agreed to go but only on the premise that he would be positioned as leader. It would have been far removed for them to deny him based on all that they were facing and unequipped to handle due to the level of opposition from their surrounding enemy.

There are numerous powerful spiritual deductions that you can make from this scenario with Jephthah, but the most profound is unlocked through the reality that:

"You Get What You Negotiate"

As a Godly leader, you should always be relying on God to lead you in the way that you need to take in order to position you in a strategic seat of conciliation. When you allow God to lead the way, the only outcome for you is to WIN!

In Jephthah stepping into his leadership role, he showed that he was spiritually fit for the position because he DID NOT RUSH into war – he handled things diplomatically when conversing with the King of Arman, explaining to him that his position on the matter was simply nothing more than a misunderstanding.

As a Godly leader, one should never make hasty decisions or take a military stance on matters with immediacy – always give an opportunity to handle things as Ambassadors of the Kingdom of God.

Always go into varying negotiations with the following:

A heart to discern the truth because everyone sitting at the table of concession's truth will always be truth to them.

A mind to understand the foundation of the matter and where it is emanating from to ensure your final decision will not bring upset but a yield to peace.

Wisdom to choose the correct God '*course of action*' and your final decision should always be based on the principles of the Word of God.

There will be times when you will encounter rebellious and disregarding people – follow the way of the Word of God in dealing with them in order to avoid being in the seat of the one bringing the offense and eventual reproach to the Kingdom of God. In other words, behave yourself and act right no matter how people may be antagonizing you.

Matthew 18:17

[17] If he pays no attention to them [refusing to listen and obey], tell it to the [a]church; and if he refuses to listen even to the church, let him be to you as a Gentile (unbeliever) and a tax collector.

Whenever you are faced with weighty and contentious matters that can affect your reputation and Ministry flow, and they will arise occasionally, never take the position of war. Have an open forum and deal with the matter. Anyone who refuses to submit to authority and causes continuous issues has to be rebuked in order to restore order, and if they persist, let them go in whatever direction they chose until they are repentant and come away from that which was intended by the enemy to destroy what God originally intended to do through your assignment.

Matthew 6:34

[34] "So do not worry about tomorrow; for tomorrow will worry about itself. Each day has enough trouble of its own.

To digest this scripture is not to infer that you are nonchalant and unconcerned about extreme and difficult situations but merely focused on God to lead you with precision so that you will not miss the minuscule details that are lost when worry sets in to confuse the mind and brings with it unnecessary mental weights.

There are over eleven places in the Bible that reference misunderstandings and their resolutions. The first position of enacting resolutions to deal with misunderstanding is to consult God the Father to get Him to weigh-in and bring equilibrium and clarity – for God is never the author of confusion – only peace.

Wait to hear God's instructions then, without any hesitation, move in obedience to accomplish what He has relayed to you. You will find that, when God "weighs-in", everything will balance itself out.

LEADERSHIP NOTES

LEADERSHIP NOTES

CHAPTER X

KEEPING YOUR VOWS

Vows are often a place of resort when faced in matters of great desperation or when someone's back is against the wall. However, vows are never to be taken lightly or without thought to being committed to the basis of the vow.

A *Vow* by definition –

A solemn promise to do or perform a specified thing, especially a deity.

The making or establishing of a vow between you and God calls for a complete and thorough evaluation of what it means to make the vow and what keeping the vow will entail prior to the issuance and confirmation of the terms of the vow.

Judges 11:30-33

30 Jephthah made a vow to the Lord and said,
"If You will indeed give the Ammonites into my hand,
31 then whatever comes out of the doors of my house to meet me when I return in peace from the Ammonites, it shall be the Lord's, and I will offer it up as a burnt offering."
32 Then Jephthah crossed over to the Ammonites to fight with them; and the Lord gave them into his hand.
33 And from Aroer to the entrance of Minnith he struck them, twenty cities, and as far as Abel-keramim (brook by the vineyard), with a very great defeat. So the Ammonites were subdued and humbled before the Israelites.

Jephthah made a vow unto God because he was faced with going into battle against a formidable enemy, the Ammonites – and he wanted an assured victory prior to going into the battle, and the way he knew how to obtain his guaranteed victory was to make a vow to the Victory Maker – God.

God is always intrigued when it comes to His people placing vows before him, vows that they promise to perform, mainly because it places the focal point on his Sovereignty as the Majestic One with all power to perform the desired outcome that the vow was predicated on.

The usual terms are:

» Lord, **IF** you do **THIS** for me…
» I **VOW** to do **THIS** for you…

Now, when we step back and look at the fact that God does not need us or anything from us, it is the other way around. It should shift our hearts to a place of humility.

You must believe that God's desire is that we win in every situation whether engaged in a battle or not. Therefore, it is of paramount importance that you come to a deeper level of understanding of all that will be required of you – before you make a vow.

Never act like 'little bad children' who will say anything just to get out of the trouble they got themselves in, and then when the trouble ends, they act like they have amnesia. The passage of scripture below shows clearly God's position on the matter.

Ecclesiastes 5:4-8

⁴ When you make a vow or a pledge to God, do not put off paying it; for God takes no pleasure in fools [who thoughtlessly mock Him]. Pay what you vow.

⁵ It is better that you should not vow than that you should vow and not pay.

⁶ Do not allow your speech to cause you to sin, and do not say before the messenger (priest) of God that it was a mistake. Why should God be angry because of your voice (words) and destroy the work of your hands?

⁷ For in a multitude of dreams and in a flood of words there is worthlessness. Rather [reverently] fear God [and worship Him with awe-filled respect, knowing who He is].

> [8] *If you see the oppression of the poor and the denial of justice and righteousness in the province, do not be shocked at the sight [of corruption]; for a higher official watches over another official, and there are higher ones over them [looking out for one another].*

When God, as the GIVER OF THE VOW, holds up His end of the negotiation, the onus then shifts to THE RECEIVER OF THE VOW to perform the remaining terms of the vow without delay. God did what you needed him to do 'on-time', so the captioned words are 'do not be late in paying'; otherwise, the Bible gives the label as a 'fool'.

When there is a delay to pay or even refusal to pay the vow, it provokes the anger of God, and He reserves the right to destroy the works of your hands. Remember, there are always consequences to breaking the terms of negotiations both in natural things and in spiritual things.

Numbers 30:2
> [2] *If a man makes a vow to the Lord or swears an oath to bind himself with a pledge [vow], he shall not break (violate, profane) his word; he shall do according to all that proceeds out of his mouth.*

Making a vow is a binding obligation from which there is no release; otherwise, there comes direct violation for which there must evolve some level of penalty or punishment.

When we examine the Psalmed writings of David, we see him making verbal affirmations that he will perform his vow to the Lord God.

Psalm 22:25
> *My praise will be of You in the great assembly. I will pay my vows [made in the time of trouble] before those who [reverently] fear Him.*

Here we see that David is in trouble and he needs a way out – he needs God to intervene and rescue him from adversarial forces and cover him from what is pursuing him. David payed his vow!

We see that David had made a vow to be a blessing to the House of God, and now when the blessings arrive, he affirms that he will pay his vow. Many people want a blessing from God, but when it is time to be a blessing out of the blessing, somehow, they feel that keeping all for themselves will be overlooked by God, but not so!

David was consistent in his performing his vows before God. Consistency gives birth to faithfulness, and God is a rewarder to those who are faithful.

Here, David expresses his openness in doing the right thing of performing his vow no matter who knows or who is watching. His heart is saying, I want the world to know that God is the one who blessed, rescued, promoted, and kept me, and to him I stand in integrity and remit my vow.

We all need to practice the principle of the Word of God in performing our vows and take no delay in doing so, just like David. David trusted God to do for him exactly what he had requested – and God did it.

LEADERSHIP NOTES

LEADERSHIP NOTES

CHAPTER XI

DANGEROUS TERMS OF YOUR VOWS

Deuteronomy 23:23

23 You shall be careful to perform that [vow] which passes your lips, just as you have made a voluntary vow to the Lord your God, just as you have promised with your own words (mouth).

Let us bring specifics to the terms on which vows are established:

» Always based on the circumstances that a person finds themselves in, usually out of desperation with limited or no other options available.

» Always given voluntarily and never under any form of coaxing or luring by the one to whom the vow is made.

» Always requires two major elements:

  » Immediate Action (Giver of Vow)

  » Performance (Receiver of Vow)

There are some people who are so spiritually shallow, not Godly leaders, of course, but those who believe they have earned the right to 'fake-it to make-it'. In other words, they try to run a scam on the Most High God, the same way they would run an emotional scam on people in their earthly sphere in order to get their way.

To produce or make a false vow is simply "to lie" about the original intention, in hope of manipulating the situation to shift it in favor of the one receiving the vow.

The best advice for those whom you may encounter after coming into the knowledge of the essentiality of performing vows is, "If you cannot fulfill the obligation of your vow – do not make it!"

In Judges 11:32, God delivered the Ammonites into Jephthah's hands and subdued his enemies under him:

Judges 11:32

[32] *Then Jephthah crossed over to the Ammonites to fight with them;*
and the Lord gave them into his hand.

Now the terms of Jephthah's vow had to be performed. The time had arrived for him to do what he initially said he would do, Verse 31…

[31] *then whatever comes out of the doors of my house to meet me when I return in peace*
from the Ammonites, it shall be the Lord's, and I will offer it up as a burnt offering."

It is most likely certain that Jephthah may have thought ahead that one of the household pets or farm wandering animals would have been the first to emerge from his house. If he had any foresight that his vow would cost him the loss of his precious virgin daughter via sacrifice of his very own terms of negotiation, in that instance, he would have never made that vow.

Advice to be noted, always proceed with caution before opening your mouth to negotiate a vow before God because you will **ALWAYS** get what you **NEGOTIATE!**

LEADERSHIP NOTES

LEADERSHIP NOTES

Chapter XII

The Power Struggle

Jephthah's vow got God to release to him an outstanding victory without the assistance, know-how, or military expertise of the Ephraimites, who denied his request to stand with him in battle against the Ammonites.

Just imagine how Jephthah must have felt about their decision to leave him to stand alone without any back-up force or accompanying alliance. The test of every Godly leader comes when you are left to bear the weight that was meant to be born by many and not just ONE.

It was because no one would stand with him that Jephthah, having no other options, sought God. Hard situations will cause you to run to God for his guidance, instruction, and direction. You will find that seeking God will cause the situation to be leveled out on an even plain field because, what you cannot handle, God will bear the extra weight with ease, but the key is call Him into the situation and give Him the seat of control.

Now after Jephthah had come into his seat of victory, the Ephraimites made it a point to have a meeting with him, not on congratulatory terms, but with divisive threats.

The truth of people's hearts are always unveiled in these types of scenarios, where they know they should have thrown their support around you and upheld you in order for you to ascend to the place where you could have conquered all with ease, but because it was not THEIR names in lights and THEY would not directly benefit, they made a decision based on the railings of their flesh that left them with regret.

The men of [the tribe of] Ephraim were summoned [to action], and they crossed over to Zaphon and said to Jephthah, "Why did you cross over to fight with the Ammonites without calling us to go with you? [For that] we will burn your house down upon you."

They did not journey with Jephthah into battle; however, they wanted to share in his victory and threaten his life and his very existence because his victory did not include them!

As you live out the call of God on your life as a Godly leader – in your innumerable encounters, there will be those that are similar or bear reference to the Ephraimites. They will know of your need of assistance in order to engage a (war) spiritual warfare situation or an actual real life hard-pressed situation, and they will refuse to assist you.

They will not be willing to take any level of risk, as far as being associated with you is concerned – whether it involves their status, position, or reputation – they will not award you their endorsement.

They will literally become enraged when God enlarges your territorial influence and give you victory where they were certain of your defeat without their involvement, and only now because they have lost the access to the place of power that would been heightened for them, had they stood with you through the trial or battle until the victory!

They will change the terms of their communication to give them an entry point to soften their stance on abandoning you when you needed them the most. They would have been more satisfied if the battle had destroyed you and not left you with one foot to stand on.

The power struggles actually begin before your battle-like situations develop, the power of influence to get people to trust your leadership and stand with you even in dire circumstances. Everyone will be available to be added to the number on bright and sunny issues, they will be the first in line, but when the battle comes with real life hard core issues that require a firm grip and wise resolve that may take all you have to conquer, there will few, if any, who will volunteer to be counted in the number.

After the battle, the power struggle speaks to those that initially opposed you. Now they want a place to bask in the light of your glorious victory, and indeed it will be glorious because God will be in it.

Judges 12:3

So when I saw that you were not coming to help me, I took my life in my hands and crossed over against the Ammonites, and the Lord handed them over to me. So why have you come up to me this day to fight against me?"

Jephthah was clear and to the point on the matter. He literally said to them,

"When I saw I could not count on you, I went to the ultimate hand of power to deliver me – God."

You must always make a mental notation that God has the ultimate and final say in all things, and as a Godly leader, you should not do anything without consulting or receiving His approval, especially in instances where you 'feel' you have it all handled.

LEADERSHIP NOTES

LEADERSHIP NOTES

CHAPTER XIII

YOUR LEADERSHIP: MEMORABLE OR FORGETTABLE

Judges 12:8-10

⁸ And after him Ibzan of Bethlehem judged Israel.
⁹ He had thirty sons, and thirty daughters whom he gave in marriage outside the family, and he brought in thirty daughters [-in-law] from outside for his sons.
He judged Israel for seven years.
¹⁰ Then Ibzan died and was buried at Bethlehem.

Here, we are introduced to the tenth leader over Israel whose life of leadership was limited to his name. Let us take a look at the name, *Izban – (Hebrew) A father or a target/ A father of coldness.*

The most notable thing spoken about him was that he was a father of an outstanding number of offspring, being thirty sons, who married off and obtained thirty daughters-in-law. And his seven-year term in office, when compared to many before him, was quite brief. He could have borne the destiny of his name and concentrated primarily on fathering his sons and raising them to be husbands and not given of himself to the position of leadership that he was given.

For many, family always comes first, and that is an awesome concept to hold fast. However, as a Godly leader, you should never abandon the assignment that God has given you or give way to displaced attention to the wrong areas. In no way is this advising to neglect family, but equilibrium is imperative to accomplish great things, as it is always God's original intention when releasing His mandate to mankind.

There was no great feat accompanied under his administration. There were no recorded writings of astounding victories for Israel during his reign, and one might ask, how effective was Izban's level of leadership?

Others might remit that he would have served a greater purpose as a leader on the home-front and not on national and governmental levels. Instead, the only thing mentioned about him, interestingly enough, he had thirty sons and thirty daughters-in-law, and that he had married them off! He had given of his best, and maybe to his family he was the greatest father of all time, but the national records did not reflect it.

National appointments should be taken seriously and never left as slight, and the selected leaders ought to do all in their power to leave the mark of achievement so that those that come behind would be able to draw knowledge and wisdom and even new concepts from what they have implemented.

He termed the marrying judge he used in his place and position to marry off all his children – then he died. There is no question to be debated here. It is blatantly obvious that his family life was more important than his leadership position, and it could be reasoned that is why his reign was cut short.

The importance of family should never be negated, as we need support in order to fulfill our God ordained purpose in the earth realm. However, we need to maintain:

»   Focus on the God assignment and positioning by seeking God for Him to use you as His toll of influence to do great exploits as you lead His people.

»   Maintain balance between the God assignment and personal/family life and social networking that have a tendency to overtake our spiritual mandates.

»   In order to do so effectively, you need to have a hand over the flesh and remain in a consecrated place where your spiritual ear is alert to the voice of God, so that you never forsake his agenda.

»   You ought to strive to be the kind of leader that is memorable, leaving a legacy of spiritual affluence to generations beyond your life span.

» Do not settle for doing the mediocre or the norm, by the book method – there are no great exploits that lead to your name being placed in the book entitled, "The Forgotten".

How do I know this is important to God? Because God himself did innumerable miraculous exploits and happenings from the beginning of time because He wants to be remembered.

Exodus 3:15

Then God also said to Moses, "This is what you shall say to the Israelites, 'The Lord, the God of your fathers, the God of Abraham, the God of Isaac, and the God of Jacob (Israel), has sent me to you.' This is My Name forever, and this is My memorial [name] to all generations.

God wants His name to be remembered...

Exodus 13:9

It shall serve as a sign to you on your hand (arm), and as a reminder on your forehead, so that the instruction (law) of the Lord may be in your mouth; for with a strong and powerful hand the Lord brought you out of Egypt.

God wants His law to be remembered...

Psalm 135:13

Your name, O Lord, endures forever, Your fame and remembrance, O Lord, [endures] throughout all generations.

God wants His fame (famous acts) to be remembered...

We have been made in God's image and likeness, and we ought to have His heart and character that says, "I am going to be great in the earth realm and fulfill my God given purpose!"

Matthew 26:6-13

[6]Now when Jesus was [back] in Bethany, at the home of [a]Simon the leper,

[7] a woman came to Him with an alabaster vial of very expensive [c]perfume and she poured it on Jesus' head as He reclined at the table.

[8] But when the [d]disciples saw it they were indignant and angry, saying, "Why all this waste [of money]?

[9] For this perfume might have been sold at a high price and the money given to the poor."

[10] But Jesus, aware [of the malice] of this [remark], said to them, "Why are you bothering the woman? She has done a good thing to Me.

[11] For you always have the poor with you; but you will not always have Me.

[12] When she poured this perfume on My body, she did it to prepare Me for burial.

[13] I assure you and most solemnly say to you, wherever this gospel [of salvation] is preached in the whole world, what this woman has done will also be told in memory of her [for her act of love and devotion]."

This scripture rehearses to us the breaking of the Alabaster Box, a box that was rare and costly, being poured on Jesus to prepare Him for what He was about to endure, and the act of what she did has been held as a memorial on her name in every generation.

It is totally up to you as a Godly leader to be one of two kinds of leader, one being Memorable, the other being Forgettable. It is your choice. God anoints and places you in a position, but it is up to you on what you choose to do with the gifts God gives you.

> **Acts 10:4**
>
> *Cornelius was frightened and stared intently at him and said, "What is it, lord (sir)?" And the angel said to him, "Your prayers and gifts of charity have ascended as a memorial offering before God [an offering made in remembrance of His past blessings].*

This scripture shows us that Cornelius, a centurion (leader of over 100 troops), a Gentile, became a memorial by how he gave his gifts of money and charity – he was Memorable!

Is your influence and leadership going to be Memorable? It is all up to you!

It is now your move!

LEADERSHIP NOTES

LEADERSHIP NOTES

CHAPTER XIV

WHEN LEADERS FOLLOW

Judges 13:3

And the [Angel of the Lord appeared to the woman and said to her, "Behold, you are infertile and have no children, but you shall conceive and give birth to a son.

There was a strategic happening that was about to occur miraculously, a heavenly announcement! A woman whose womb was tightly shut in barrenness was about to conceive.

This was a magnanimous happening based on the purpose for which the child was to be born. The child was to be one chosen by God to deliver Israel out of the hands of their enemies, the Philistines.

One would think that with such important news, God would have spoken directly to Manoah, who was **the leader** in his household. But instead, the Angel of the Lord appeared to Manoah's wife – the one whom he led. She brought the profound message to him verbatim; she did not leave out any detail, and she relayed it exactly the way the Angel gave it to her, and all of this happened when she was not even expecting such a visitation.

God always chooses specified times to reveal His divine plan and purpose through angelic visitation. Whenever he does, it is an indicator that he wants to do something beyond the norm in the earth realm.

The Angel entrusted her with in-depth details of how she was to handle her pregnancy as well as the purpose of the child that her womb would be opened to carry. According to verse 6, it was this woman who had carried the message of the angelic announcement to her husband.

And this proves, you do not need a name or title for God to use you... Let me use this moment to share a personal experience. It may bring clarity to the depth of this chapter.

Years ago, I found myself engaged to a young 'man of God' who loved the special privileges that were afforded to him with the title that he carried as an Apostle. He was full of pride, and I was told by someone in his family that he carried a mentality that men were superior to women and served only minor purposes when it came to the Church.

Well, one day, we happened to be at a local mid-day prayer meeting together, and the Prophetess W. (we will call her) released a prophetic word over my life that I would be used by God, and I would travel the world to carry the gospel. It was not until after this happening that I began to see another side of him. He started making sarcastic comments, and it escalated to condescending implications, and in one of those instances, he said to me, "God made man first, so God speaks to man not woman. Who do you think you are, all over the place prophesying? Y'all women are not worth a cup of spit." It was in that moment I realized that this man WAS NOT THE ONE!

Many people feel a level of superiority over others based on the title or position they hold, and they oftentimes resort to emitting this kind of treatment on others.

This should not be indicative of spiritual leaders on any level from the novice to the elder.

Over the centuries, God has used many men and women to accomplish His purpose and perform great exploits on behalf of the Kingdom of God, and amazingly enough, many of them remained nameless. To not be named or given specific recognition does not say the person was not a vital component or they were in any way insignificant. It is simply saying that God wanted to be the ONE pronounced as the catalyst in the enzyme reaction; in other words, He wanted to get the Glory out of the situation.

Manoah was named in this Chapter, and he was the leader in his family, yet God did not give him the allowance to be the first recipient of the message. It was obvious in his prayer that he received the message and was anxious to be taught personally what needed to be done concerning the birth of his long awaited son.

The Bible says that God listened to Manoah, and for the second time, the Angel appeared to the woman and not Manoah.

Manoah had to 'follow' his wife's lead to the place where the Angel first appeared to her alone. So why did the Angel appear to the woman (wife) vs. Manoah? It all had to do with the perceptions of the heart.

Manoah's perception was dull to null. He had not even realized that the person he was offering food to was an Angel, who of course, does not need earthly food sustenance. Yet, the perception of his wife's heart was pure and open, which enabled her to be chosen for an angelic visitation – not once, but twice.

The perception of a Godly leader's heart must be pure so as not to be passed over for those who are ready to receive the message from God. Otherwise, they will forever be left to follow those that they were called to lead.

Think for a moment of leaders being left in the dark or being placed on the list as the last to know when it comes to the details that they should be privy to first as the leader. This could prove to be an uncomfortable position.

Manoah was more interested in the futuristic occupation of the child that was to be born, the answer to which was referred to, what was already spoken to the woman – to be a deliverer over the nation of Israel.

When God entrusts a message to someone, it is because He trusts the heart of the messenger to deliver it exactly the way He sent it!

Let me encourage you, Godly leader. Hold your heart pure before God, so He can trust you with life changing, dimension shifting, and world impacting messages that the nations are waiting to hear.

Psalm 51:10

Create in me a clean heart, O God; And renew a right and steadfast spirit within me.

Here, we see David crying out before God for a clean heart. He understood the importance of staying connected to God, the plug-in is purity. We can deduct from this scripture why clearly David was named 'a man after God's own heart.' When your heart is pure, it will position you to have such intimacy relationally with God – Heart to Heart.

> ### Psalm 26:2
> *Examine me, O Lord, and try me; Test my heart and my mind.*

Again, David was putting himself before God's hand to be examined and evaluated to see whether he was ready for God to use him before he launched out. So many leaders launch out prematurely and cause cataclysmic, even catastrophic, things to happen because they were not ready.

Most people want to sit in the seat of leadership because it seems to carry such power, and indeed it does, but more importantly, it carries the heavy weight of responsibility, for which there must come alignment in accountability.

As you hold your place of purity – your heart's perception will be open to receive from God, and you will not have to be set in line to *follow* those you have been called to *lead*.

LEADERSHIP NOTES

LEADERSHIP NOTES

CHAPTER XV

GODLY LEADERS ADHERE TO GODLY COUNSEL

Judges 14:2

So, he went back and told his father and his mother, "I saw a woman in Timnah, one of the daughters of the Philistines; now get her for me as a wife."

Now, it is time to talk about Samson, the strongest man to have ever lived during his time, when the Spirit of the Lord came upon him. For Samson, it all came down to "what he saw." His eyes found delight, and thereafter, his heart yearned for a woman of the Philistine heritage, which was not formally permitted among his people.

The Philistines were a people who were literally uncircumcised (the foreskin of their men were not removed as was the custom of the Israelites), and to intermarry with them would be the same as to accept in homage aspects of their culture and religious beliefs.

Even though there was no formal law written against Samson marrying the Philistine woman, his parents tried their best to dissuade him from doing so and offered to him good Godly counsel. They went as far as to detail the option of choosing a wife from among his own people.

When you are striving to live a life that pleases God, Godly leaders should never ignore the objections and/or advice of the wise counsel that God has placed in your life because it is their eyes of knowledge and wisdom that can see what you cannot see. Adhering to good Godly counsel can save your life from "Destiny-Interruptus."

Nevertheless, Samson was insistent that his parents perform whatever was necessary to acquire the young woman to become his wife. His instructions were blatant and bold in defiance. "Go get her!" were Samson's last words to them on the matter.

How could they tell their spoiled, miracle gift, and only child, "No"? They had to comply with his demand because they loved him beyond measure. But they should have loved him enough to be as bold to him as he was to them and rebut with "No is no!" Yet, all of these happenings were aligning Samson with the will of God and positioning him amid his enemies. This is called – **The Art of War**.

Samson was a God ordained leader from birth, and he was endowed with God given authority that even his parents submitted to as it is clearly seen.

This verse gives us the prime directive behind why God allowed Samson to develop the overwhelming desire he had within to marry the Philistine woman. God had a plan to infiltrate the Philistine borders, and he was going to marry Samson into the nation and its people.

"It was of the Lord"

This burning passion to have by his nation's guidelines; he should not have emanated from God's plan to get into the borders of the enemy camp just so he could issue an Executive Order to move against them and destroy them as a nation.

This is one very pertinent reason that submission to a leader (as Samsons' parents were to him) is vital because God might truly be behind the situation with plans to manifest

His divine purpose. Always remember that the leader is first accountable to God and will bear the judgement if they acted outside of the Will of God, not the person who submits to their leader – they are free from inclusion.

God's plan was to remove the hold of the Philistine hand as the oppressive power over His people and restore dominion to His people, Israel.

Judges 14:5-6

[5] *Then Samson went down to Timnah with his father and mother [to arrange the marriage], and they came as far as the vineyards of Timnah; and [a]suddenly, a young lion came roaring toward him.*

[6] *The Spirit of the Lord came upon him mightily, and he tore the lion apart as one tears apart a young goat, and he had nothing at all in his hand; but he did not tell his father or mother what he had done.*

Samson had an encounter where he had slain a ferocious lion when the Spirit of the Lord came upon him. And it was this experience that he composed a riddle to which only he knew the answer.

Thus, after the wedding ceremony was over and Samson had been accepted by the Philistines, he told them his composed riddle and with it the rules and the prize of the winnings. The bet was 30 Linen Garments and 30 Changes of Clothing!

Samson was beyond sure that he would end up the winner – after all, he was the only one who knew the answer.

As a Godly leader, never follow Samson and put yourself in a place to "bite off more than you can chew" in any situation because you may find that you may end up choking in your trying to win.

The spirit of competition often rises when one feels the need to outshine others, and this spirit is attached to selfish ambition that wants only conceited desires that will lead to leadership downfall.

Within Judges 14, we see that, on one side, Samson was overly confident, but on the other side, those to whom the riddle had been presented had made up their minds that they would win "by any means necessary."

> ### Judges 14:15
>
> *Then on the fourth day they said to Samson's wife, "Persuade your husband to tell us [through you] the [answer to the] riddle, or we will burn you and your father's household with fire. Have you invited us to make us poor? Is this not true?"*

These persons went to the extent of threatening Samson's wife and coerced her to work behind the scenes to probe her husband for the answer to the riddle so that, at the end of the day, they could be called the winners over Samson.

As you are reading, do not take this poignant lesson for granted. Always walk in wisdom and discernment because there are people who are devised by the hand of the enemy to undermine you and undercut the win that God has designed for you.

It took seven days for her to wear Samson down and retrieve the information from him.

The most poignant premise cited here for every Godly leader is, when God gives you a perfectly created composition (a personal word/vital insider information), do not share it with anyone – no matter how they probe.

For Samson, he gave into the pressure of his wife's request, and she brought against him the ultimate weapon – the dagger of betrayal. She took that answer and ran to the ones who had threatened to destroy everything that her family owned. She saved their house but lost her husband. Samson could not even handle looking at her after what she had done. He had to battle through the internal turmoil of dealing with betrayal by his wife.

In every case of disloyalty and distrust, there is a pattern that leads to the death of the relationship. There are some things that a relationship just cannot live through without God's hand being involved. And there are many times that, even after time has passed and there is forgiveness, things regarding that relationship are never quite the same.

As a result of Samson's loss, he was now in a "choke-hold" situation and had to perform his end of the bargain. Samson ended up killing the men of Ashkelon in order to take from them their apparel to satisfy the prize terms of the competition.

Here is some advice for all Godly leaders. Run from all level of competition, especially competition in Ministry. Competition in Ministry can develop scenarios of hurt on so many levels. Whenever you see it evolving, address it in prayer but also expose it and put a "spiritual head-lock" on it and "take it down!"

LEADERSHIP NOTES

LEADERSHIP NOTES

CHAPTER XVI

DON'T LOSE IT

We know that Samson was a mighty warrior, if not to say, the most notable one of his time, and that he had been endowed with a unique ability and specialized skills of extraordinary strength.

Although he had great strength, he lacked wisdom and had an apparent weakness in the area of his flesh geared toward, "lust of the eyes." He had overwhelming desires to quell the fires of his sexual passions of his flesh that eventually led to the descent of his leading the nation of Israel.

Judges 16:1

Then Samson went to Gaza and saw a prostitute there, and went in to her.

He was a man of great physical power and strength, but he had obviously lost his devotion to God by seeking solace of the flesh to a woman of the night.

The trend of any Godly leader should never lead to the place where the flesh and its ungodly desires take precedence over the call of God or the mandate that has to be fulfilled. The flesh has a way of taking over and causing an immediate downward spiral that will lead to utter destruction.

Proverbs 14:12

There is a way which seems right to a man and appears straight before him,
But its end is the way of death.

That which appears to be seemingly right outside of God's leadership, guidance, or instructions will cause total disruption in areas where there should have been a seamless victory or transition.

Whenever the flesh is allowed to elevate and stand in "first place" over what God had originally spoken or purposed to be done, at that point, it becomes obvious that the things of God have been disregarded, which displaces loyalty and commitment – total loss of devotion to God.

Where there is a loss of dedication, it leads to:

» Being easily deceived by lies and overcome by hard-pressed words becoming subject to enemy tactics, when it should be the other way around.

Who Samson was in strength was directly linked to the secret behind his strength, which meant that God never intended anyone to know the secret; otherwise, it would have defeated the purpose. When you release information to the enemy, never be naïve to believe that the enemy will not turn around and use that information against you to gain the tactical advantage over you to profit or advance.

There are specifics about your life and call that God never wants certain people privy at all or whatsoever; for this main reason, He has foreknowledge as Sovereign God of what the intention of those persons will be should they attain such information.

Remember, the flesh will always be driven to do evil and that which is contrary to the Divine Law or God's way. Therefore, give it no room or space to advance. The flesh causes yielding to sin easy, and we know that the power of leaven (sin) takes over incredibly fast.

Galatians 5:8-9

[8] *This [deceptive] persuasion is not from Him who called you [to freedom in Christ].*
[9] *A little leaven [a slight inclination to error] leavens the whole batch*
[it perverts the concept of faith and misleads the church].

If you never fulfill your God given potential because the flesh became the governing factor, as a result, there comes a loss of the Anointing because your sin disconnected you from the source of your power.

Judges 16:15-24

¹⁵ Then she said to him, "How can you say, 'I love you,' when your heart is not with me? You have mocked me these three times and have not told me where your great strength lies."

¹⁶ When she pressured him day after day with her words and pleaded with him, he was annoyed to death.

¹⁷ Then [finally] he told her everything that was in his heart and said to her, "A razor has never been used on my head, for I have been a Nazirite to God from my mother's womb. If I am shaved, then my strength will leave me, and I will become weak and be like any [other] man."

¹⁸ Then Delilah realized that he had told her everything in his heart, so she sent and called for the Philistine lords, saying, "Come up this once, because he has told me everything in his heart." Then the Philistine lords came up to her and brought the money [they had promised] in their hands.

¹⁹ She made Samson sleep on her knees, and she called a man and had him shave off the seven braids of his head. Then she began to abuse Samson, and his strength left him.

²⁰ She said, "The Philistines are upon you, Samson!" And he awoke from his sleep and said, "I will go out as I have time after time and shake myself free." For Samson did not know that the Lord had departed from him.

²¹ Then the Philistines seized him and gouged out his eyes; and they brought him down to Gaza and bound him with [two] bronze chains; and he was forced to be a grinder [of grain into flour at the mill] in the prison.

²² But the hair of his head began to grow again after it had been shaved off.

²³ Now the Philistine lords gathered together to offer a great sacrifice to Dagon their god, and to celebrate, for they said, "Our god has given Samson our enemy into our hands!"

²⁴ When the people saw Samson, they praised their god, for they said, "Our god has handed over our enemy to us, The ravager of our country, Who has killed many of us."

Samson lost his strength and his leadership position of prominence and with it his opportunity to maximize his potential in the earth realm. Samson never fulfilled his God assignment by God's design. The element of sin intervened and shortchanged how everything was to be done.

Sin can change the trajectory of your life! Keep the leaven of sin out of every aspect of your life and watch God elevate you and use you in levels and arenas far beyond your wildest dreams.

God has created everyone with a distinctive design, and He wants us to fulfil the mission and/or assignment that He has planned. He wants us to go to the full journey and not to fall or fail in the middle or falter in the end!

Samson ended up dying disabled and defeated by his enemies because he did not silence and put in subjection the passionate cravings and yearnings of his flesh, and because he did not handle his matters with discretion, he could not trust himself to keep the secret of his life's success.

Proverbs 2:11

Discretion will preserve you; Understanding will guard you.

In this walk with God, you do not have the liberty of casting your pearls before swine and naively believing that they will not be trampled underfoot. Learn from Samson's mistakes and maximize all the power and gifts that God has given you and position yourself as a Global Impactor and change nations for the advance of the Kingdom of God.

Don't lose your Anointing through the infiltration of sin and be left defenseless against the enemy's attack, not even realizing that God has left the building (you as the temple).

Judges 16:20

She said, "The Philistines are upon you, Samson!" And he awoke from his sleep and said, "I will go out as I have time after time and shake myself free." For Samson did not know that the Lord had departed from him.

The Spirit of the Lord – the power and anointing of God had left Samson. The secret was out, which gave Samson's enemies the tactical advantage for the first time in his life. He lost to his enemies, and it was only because his defense system was no longer in place.

God's power that was vested in Samson was gone.

Remember Godly leaders, without God and without God's power, you are absolutely nothing!

John 15:4-5

[4]Remain in Me, and I [will remain] in you. Just as no branch can bear fruit by itself without remaining in the vine, neither can you [bear fruit, producing evidence of your faith] unless you remain in Me.
[5] I am the Vine; you are the branches. The one who remains in Me and I in him bears much fruit, for [otherwise] apart from Me [that is, cut off from vital union with Me] you can do nothing.

Galatians 6:3

For if anyone thinks he is something, when he is nothing, he deceives himself.

As a Godly leader, you must NEVER divert from God's original intent regarding your call. Stay with the leading of the Holy Spirit; he will lead and guide you into all truth – always.

Second, never allow yourself as a Godly leader to get caught up in the moment of your success. Instead, be ever cognizant of God's power that is powering you. Find your heart in a confident place to rely fully and completely on God and not your flesh.

The flesh will always lead you to error in judgment.

Third, never ignore the areas in your character or your life that either are or can become detrimental if left unattended with no repair or removal.

Focus on those areas and address them so that you can become empowered to subdue it before it overpowers you.

Call in the supernatural reinforcement strength of God, and God will show up and give you victory in those areas of your life!

Keep yourself constantly on your personal altar before God, being careful to empty out everything in, on, or around you that can hinder what God wants to do through you. You have been created by and for God and His ultimate divine purpose.

LEADERSHIP NOTES

LEADERSHIP NOTES

BIOGRAPHY

OF

APOSTLE PROPHETESS ROCHELLE GRAHAM

A postle Rochelle Graham is an anointed, poised, powerful prophetically gifted preacher/teacher of the Word of God, who was born in the beautiful archipelago of Islands in the Commonwealth of the Bahamas, where she completed her tertiary level of education in the early 1990's. It was September 1993 that she gave her life completely to the Lord and became an active member on the Evangelistic Team at Bahamas Christian Fellowship Ministries International under the leadership of well-known Dr. Apostle Paul Butler.

After serving for a number of years, Apostle Graham was led by the Spirit of the Lord to begin to enjoin herself to Temple Fellowship Ministries, where the prophetic gifting on her life was strengthened and enhanced under Master Prophet Bishop Kirkwood Murphy. She remained faithful to the call of God and continued to seek the Lord for his perfect will concerning her life and destiny.

In Apostle Graham seeking the Lord, it led to her divine connection to Master Prophet Apostle Demarco D. Grant in the year 2000, who took time to train her in the areas of new dimensions of prayer and deliverance while at the Lily of The Valley Deliverance Ministries International. She was trained over the span of three (3) years in the spirit of excellence for ministry protocol, family counseling, and prophetic deliverance and demonic expulsion.

Spiritual promotion was established in her life in the year 2004, when she was ordained and installed as the Assistant Pastor at the Healing Hands Prayer and Deliverance Ministries under the late Apostle Prophetess Charlene Duncombe. Apostle Graham served faithfully and established many in-house conferences and local outreach events. She was blessed to travel extensively during that time into the local family of islands as well as into the United States of America.

In 2011, God spoke to Apostle Graham and gave her unction to commence her very own prayer ministry, namely, Righteous Remnant Ministries International – which encompasses a full weekly array of powerful prayer services and community outreach as well as a local assembly that is expanding daily and operating in the fivefold ministry, which has now expanded to the North Carolina, U.S.A., where she was blessed with love in marriage to Bishop Brian J. Graham.

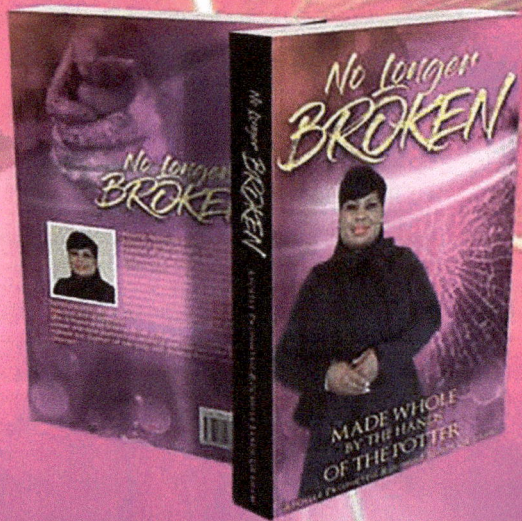

www.ingramcontent.com/pod-product-compliance
Lightning Source LLC
Chambersburg PA
CBHW051311020426
42333CB00027B/3299